THE
YOU AND ME
HERITAGE TREE

THE YOU AND ME HERITAGE TREE

BY PHYLLIS FIAROTTA AND NOEL FIAROTTA

CHILDREN'S CRAFTS FROM 21 AMERICAN TRADITIONS

WORKMAN PUBLISHING COMPANY, INC. NEW YORK

Library of Congress Cataloging in Publication Data

Fiarotta, Phyllis.
  The you and me heritage tree craft book for children.

  *SUMMARY: Step-by-step instructions for more than 100 craft
projects drawn from twenty-two different ethnic traditions in the
United States and using easily available materials.*
  1. Handicraft—Juvenile literature. [1. Handicraft]
I. Fiarotta, Noel, joint author. II. Title.
TT160.F52 1976   745.5   75-44133
ISBN 0-911104-74-7
ISBN 0-911104-73-9 pbk.

Illustrations: Phyllis Fiarotta
Book Designer: Bernard Springsteel
Cover Design: Paul Hanson
Cover Illustration: Tom Cook
Photographs: Ray Solwinski

Workman Publishing Company, Inc.
231 East 51 Street
New York, New York 10022

Manufactured in the United States of America
First printing June 1976
1 3 5 7 9 8 6 4 2

Dedicated to our Mom and Dad who gave us a resplendent heritage

CONTENTS

1. HISTORIES 23

6. PAINT 171

7. PAPER 193

8. YARN 227

FOREWORD TO PARENTS

The You And Me Heritage Tree contains crafts of twenty-one of the ethnic, national or native groups which settled in this land. It is a book of family heritages, of Grandma's faded picture weaving or Grandpa's burnt-bowl corncob pipe. Every group has its craftwork legacy, a proud history of handmade things. Now your children may share this tradition by making the craft projects themselves. They will learn not only about their own cultural roots but those of all the people who made America their home.

This book belongs to the heirs of all Americans, the youth of today. It was written for children to understand. All specific measurements (inches and feet) are omitted, leaving the total creative process to the young craftsperson. Drawings accompany each craft project, and in some cases, step-by-step illustrations are included. No guesswork is needed.

Not all crafts in this book will appeal to your children. Don't force them, just for creativity's sake, to make something they won't enjoy. Let them decide which projects interest them most. Your children know themselves very well and what it is they most want to make.

The adult plays an important part in the construction process. Read through this book before you hand it over to your children. Look at all the craft items and see how the instructions are written. *You will notice the symbol ** in front of a direction. This means that potentially dangerous household equipment is called for, or that the execution of the step so marked may be too difficult for a child.* It is advisable for you to supervise this activity. Keep in mind your children's physical abilities and limitations. If you feel they cannot perform a particular task, you will have to do it for them. Allow youngsters to feel, however, that they are the ones creating the objects, even though it is you who have just bored a hole in a piece of cardboard or cut a length of string.

Every craft item in this book is presented in four parts: the drawing, the instructions, symbol and text indicating the project's ethnic background, and a list of craft materials. Encourage your children to read through the instructions several times before they begin, and study the drawings carefully. You will provide them with the necessary craft supplies and help them gather any natural materials needed. Craft supplies can be bought in a stationery or art supply store, or at the stationery counter of department stores. You will probably have many of the supplies you will need in your own home.

There may be a dozen or more families of different national or ethnic background on the street where you live. Each family has its own cultural heritage. Your children play with your neighbor's children, and all share in each other's customs and traditions. The crafts in this book are just one part of a people's legacy. By working the crafts your children will learn more about the people who not only live in their neighborhood but their country.

JUST FOR YOU

The United States of America did not become the great nation it is in just a few short days. It took several centuries of exploration, war, and settlement to make it happen. America represents the saga of people leaving their homelands in search of a better life. Hard work was the rule. It was only during the treasured hours of relaxation that the tired settlers could make items for the home and crude toys for the children.

The You And Me Heritage Tree contains many of the fascinating crafts worked by settlers as well as those of native Americans, the Indians. Some crafts were made by people long before their arrival in America or the arrival of the first settlers. Others were born in America and can be found in no other place. All are handed down to you by an adventurous group of people, people who were your forebears. Some time ago your distant relatives helped lay down the cornerstone of this nation.

Look through the book and decide which craft item you would like to make first. It might be a corn husk doll or an Indian clay-coil bowl. It is very important that you read all the directions, not just once, but several times before you begin. If there is something you don't understand, have someone explain it to you. It is important that you study the drawings as well. You will be better able to understand the directions if you see how a craft is put together. The symbol beginning each project indicates what group originated the craft.

Ask your Mom and Dad for help if you feel it is necessary. They will buy and help you find all the materials you will need for the projects you choose. If you have difficulty cutting, threading, sewing, or doing anything, ask for a helping hand. Once you learn the proper way to handle tools and materials, the construction of the items will be easier.

It is now your turn to discover Americans through their crafts. Once you begin discovering, you'll probably find it difficult to stop. Your heritage crafts will take you into the lives of many different Americans. The journey should be fun and rewarding.

THINGS YOU'LL NEED FOR EACH CHAPTER

Here you'll find listed those materials which are particularly applicable to each chapter. Of course, materials listed under a given chapter may be required for another.

CHAPTER 2—BEADS

• **Seed beads** are tiny glass beads sometimes referred to as Indian beads. They are sold in five-and-ten-cent stores and at sewing counters. They come in all colors and in small packages.

• **Tube beads** are elongated plastic beads with a large openings. They are sold in packages in craft stores.

• **Round beads** come in wood, plastic, and many other materials. They are sold in packages at sewing centers and craft shops and usually have small openings. The best source for round beads is your Mom's old, broken necklaces.

• **Macaroni beads** are actually pieces of small tube macaroni that look like seed beads. Macaroni beads can be dyed in cups of food coloring and water. After coloring, dry the macaroni on paper towels.

CHAPTER 3—EGGS

• **Chicken eggs** are the most popular eggs in America. You can also use duck eggs and empty eggs found in the woods for your craftwork.

• **Plastic eggs** can be bought around Easter time. They are sold at the five-and-ten-cent store.

• **Dyes for eggs** can be bought during the Easter season. Follow package directions for egg-dyeing.

• **Fabric dyes** or **food coloring** are also used to color eggs, and can be bought all year round. Dilute the dye or coloring in water to the intensity of color desired.

CHAPTER 4—FABRIC

• **Felt** is a strong, heavy fabric that comes in many colors. It is sold in small squares. It can be glued to a surface with liquid white glue.

• **Scrap fabric** is odds and ends of cloth that your Mom saves from her sewing projects. You can cut up old clothes to make scrap fabric.

- **Netting** is a fabric with the cross threads of its weave so far apart you can see through them. It is sold at sewing centers.

CHAPTER 5—NATURE

- **Corn** is a valuable craft material. It can be bought fresh on-the-cob, in late summer and early autumn. In some stores fresh corn is sold most of the year. Save the husks and cobs. You can also buy frozen corn-on-the-cob at your grocery store.

- **Straw** is available from old wisk and sweeping brooms.

- **Apples** are available all year 'round, especially during the autumn months.

- **Pine cones** are the seed carriers of pine trees. Other trees grow cones too—like the larch and the spruce. The next time you pass a pine, spruce, or larch, look under the tree for fallen cones.

- **Prunes, potatoes,** and **chestnuts** can be purchased at your supermarket. Chestnuts have a short season, usually the autumn months.

- **Hickory nuts** and **acorns** can be gathered in the forest during the early autumn.

- **Sand** is found at the seashore or in the desert. It can be bought at the hardware store or at the florist's.

- **Shells** are best found by the seashore. Clams, oysters, and other shellfish can be bought at the fish market or in large supermarkets; enjoy eating them and then save the shells. Restaurants that specialize in seafood dinners also have a good supply of shells which should be available for the asking. Florist's and hobby stores sell packages of pretty shells, and there are the newer shell shops which carry all kinds of shells exclusively.

CHAPTER 6—PAINT

- **Poster paints** are paints that can be removed from your hands with water. They come in many colors and are sold in jars.

- **Watercolor paints** are little tablets of hard color that must be daubed with a wet brush to use. The paints come in a tin which has at least six colors in it.

- **Colored felt-tipped markers** are tubes or "pencils" of enclosed ink with a felt coloring tip. They can take the place of paint in some cases. There are two kinds of felt-tipped markers. Indelible markers do not wash out with water. Watercolor markers will smudge if they come in contact with water.

- **Watercolor paint brushes** are brushes meant to be used for watercolor artwork and come in many sizes. The larger brushes are used to paint in large areas. The smaller brushes are used to paint in small designs.

CHAPTER 7—PAPER

- **White drawing paper** is important in craft projects as well as for drawing. Drawing paper is heavy, smooth paper that comes in pads or packages.

• **Colored construction paper** is heavy paper that comes in many wonderful colors. The sheets are sold in packages, and many paper sizes are available. Try to pick the correct size for the craft you will be making. Save all large scraps in a box or bag. You never know when you might need a little bit of color.

• **Tracing paper** is very light, transparent paper. When it is placed on a drawing, you can see the drawing through it. Tracing paper comes in pads and is very important for many of your craft projects.

• **Typewriter paper** is a white paper that is lighter than white drawing paper but heavier than tracing paper. You can see a drawing under it. It comes in packaged sheets.

• **Cardboard** is very heavy paper. You can find it tucked in shirts which come from the laundry or in packages of new clothes. Other boxes found around the house—like shoe and hat boxes—are made of it. Cardboard may also be bought in art supply stores. Save all pieces of cardboard you find in your home.

• **Corrugated cardboard** is brown cardboard that many cartons are made of. It is a sandwich of a ripply center paper glued between two sheets of heavy brown paper. You can see through two edges.

• **Oaktag,** sometimes called poster board, is a light cardboard and is sold at stationery, art, and some five-and-ten-cent stores. It is available in white as well as in a wide variety of colors.

• **Colored tissue paper** is lightweight paper that you can see through. It comes in all the colors of the rainbow and is sold in packages at stationery or art supply stores. It is easy to fold and cut.

• **Origami paper** is a lightweight paper sold in novelty stores. You can buy packages or small squares of Origami paper in many different colors. This paper is colored on one side and white on the other.

• **Mat board** is heavy cardboard sold at art supply or stationery stores in large sheets. One side is white and the other side is a cream color. It can have either a smooth or bumpy surface.

CHAPTER 8—YARN

• **Knitting Yarn** is soft wool or synthetic yarn which comes in many colors. You can buy small skeins at sewing centers or you may find small scraps in your Mom's knitting box.

• **Embroidery thread** is thinner than knitting yarn and is made of cotton. It is available in a wide variety of colors and sold in small packages at sewing centers.

• **Cord** comes in many thicknesses and is usually white or a natural light brown in color. Kite string is considered thin cord and rope a thick cord. Cord is available at stationery or hardware stores.

SUPPLIES YOU'LL NEED FOR ALL CHAPTERS

GLUES AND PASTE

• **Liquid white glue** comes in plastic bottles with applicator tips. This glue makes a strong bond when it dries. Many projects require a glue with an applicator-tip bottle for drawing fine glue lines.

• **Liquid brown glue,** or mucilage, comes in a bottle with a rubber cap that is used for spreading. It is a light adhesive.

• **Paper paste** is a white thick adhesive. It usually comes in a jar, and has a plastic spreader. Paper paste is best for sticking paper to paper.

• **Stick glues** are glues that come in the form of long sticks which are rubbed on the surface to be glued. They are best used for sticking paper to paper.

CRAFT TOOLS

• A **compass** is a device used to make a perfect circle. It has two arms, one pointed and one holding a pencil. The compass opens and closes, and you can draw any size circle you need with it. Ask Mom or Dad how to use a compass if you don't know.

• **Paper punchers** are used to make holes in paper and lightweight cardboard. These holes are the size of those punched in looseleaf paper. To make a hole, a piece of paper is inserted in the puncher which is squeezed and released.

HOW TO TRANSFER PATTERNS

The patterns in this book are drawn with a heavier line than the other illustrations. Instructions about patterns will always be given along with the directions·on making the craft.

TO TRACE A PATTERN

1. Place a sheet of tracing paper over the page that has the pattern you wish to trace, Fig. a.

2. Follow the outline of the pattern with a soft pencil on the tracing paper. Do not press hard or you will see pencil marks on the page.

3. After you have traced the pattern on tracing paper, cut it out with your scissors, Fig. b.

4. Put the new cutout pattern on the paper you wish to use, Fig. c.

5. With a pencil, trace around the edge of the cutout pattern, Fig. c.

6. Remove the cutout pattern and cut out the new drawing from the paper. Now you are ready to continue with your project, Figs. d and e.

TO TRANSFER A PATTERN WITH A PENCIL RUBBING

1. Place a sheet of tracing paper over the page that has the pattern you wish to transfer.

2. Follow the outline of the pattern with a soft pencil, Fig. a.

3. After you have traced the pattern from the book, turn the tracing paper over, and rub along the back of the tracing outline with the side of the pencil lead. Make sure the back-and-forth scribbling covers all of the pattern outline, Fig. f.

4. Place the tracing over the paper you wish to use, scribbled side down, Fig. g.

5. Draw over the lines of the original tracing with a pencil. Press hard on the line as you draw. The rubbing will act like carbon paper.

6. Lift up the tracing paper.

7. The lead that you scribbled on the back of the tracing paper will have come off on the paper where you drew with your pencil, Fig. h.

TO TRANSFER A PATTERN WITH CARBON PAPER

1. Buy a package of carbon paper at the five-and-ten-cent or stationery store. Carbon paper is paper with a layer of blue or black coloring on one side. It is used for making duplicate copies on a typewriter.

2. Trace the patterns from the book onto tracing paper with a pencil.

3. Place a sheet of carbon paper with the carbon side down onto a sheet of paper.

4. Place the tracing over the carbon paper.

5. Draw over the lines of the original tracing with a pencil. Press hard.

6. Remove the tracing and the carbon paper. A carbon drawing will be transferred onto the bottom paper.

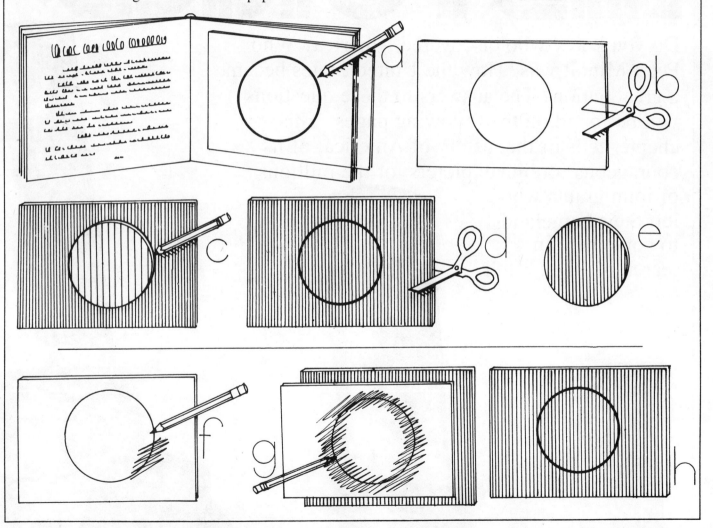

21

HISTORIES

Do you know who discovered America? Who Peter Minuit was? How the United States became a great nation? The answers to these questions will be found on the following pages. This chapter tells of the history of America; of its courageous foreign explorers; of the millions of immigrants who left their homelands to come here in search of a better life.

COLUMBUS AND THE OTHER FIRST EXPLORERS

Although he was not the first to "discover" America, Christopher Columbus is the most famous explorer of the New World. He had the then wild idea that the world was round, not flat. Columbus went to Spain and visited King Ferdinand and Queen Isabella. He told them that he could sail to India by traveling west. He wanted to find a new route that would open the spice trade. Columbus received three ships and a crew.

In 1492, the Santa Maria, the Pinta, and the Nina sailed from Palos. On October 12 Columbus landed in San Salvador and thought it was India. He named the people he met there Indians. The land was claimed for Spain, and he returned home. Columbus made several other voyages but never stepped foot on North American soil.

The news of a New World spread over Spain and to other European countries.

The Dutch, French, English and Spanish were sailing neck and neck to claim new land for their countries.

When cities popped up along the Atlantic coast, settlers, not explorers, arrived. This was the end of the ship-sailing explorer and America, west of the thirteen colonies, was explored on foot. A new group of adventurous men emerged, and these men led the nationwide settlement of what became the United States.

AFRICAN

TRUMPETS The rhythms and songs of the African culture created a new music in America, jazz. It is America's most famous, original music.

The first African people arrived in America in 1619. They didn't come as free people. They were brought to be slaves and sold to plantation owners. They worked long, hard hours for very few rewards.

For the next one hundred and eighty-nine years, most African people came to America as slaves. January 1, 1863 was a happy day. On it, Abraham Lincoln signed the Emancipation Proclamation. This law abolished slavery. Now the immigrants from Africa became citizens of the United States.

Black people learned many skills on the plantations that would be of use to them. Many became blacksmiths, furniture makers, and tailors. Others became fine musicians. It was the black musicians who combined the rhythms of Africa with the spiritual songs they used to sing on the plantations to form a new style of music. It was in New Orleans that black musicians first played this jazz.

The African people have contributed greatly to America. Jazz is only one of the black people's great contributions.

CHINESE

LANTERN A burning candle inside a hanging lantern brings mystery and life to homes and to festive celebrations.

The Gold Rush of 1848 brought people from the East coast to California. Large seaports opened in the West and ships began sailing to mysterious China. Yankee sailors told tall tales of mountains of gold in America.

Chinese men worked in the gold mines, but found very little gold. Since there was very little work for them, most went back to China. Those that did remain worked at different jobs. Some were servants for miners, and a large number helped build the Central Pacific Railroad.

Chinese people settled in communities with their own people. The communities are called Chinatowns. They often have beautiful temples in them and, of course, lots of restaurants. A Chinatown is a place to buy a bamboo backscratcher, a honeycomb fan, or a bag of fortune cookies.

CZECHOSLOVAKIAN

FLOWERING HEART This is the traditional Czechoslovakian design which was embroidered on many costumes. It is the sign of eternal love.

Augustine Herrman was one of the first Czechoslovakians to see what America was all about. He arrived in New Amsterdam in the early 1600's and finally settled in Maryland. Augustine bought a large tract of land that he called Bohemia Manor. Other Bohemians (for Bohemia was the name of that part of eastern Europe from which the Czechs first came) settled near his estate.

Czechoslovakian people didn't want to leave their homeland in large numbers until 1840. It seems that a severe drought dried up the soil in Bohemia. Farmers couldn't grow a stalk of golden wheat or a hearty potato. The drought forced thousands of Czechs to immigrate to America.

Kutna Hora, a farmer, led the first group of Czechoslovakian people to America. They set up the first Czechoslovakian farming community in Wisconsin. Like most groups, the Czechs set up their own communities and helped each other in times of need.

DUTCH

TULIP The Dutch are famous for their tulips. This flower is the prize of every garden in Holland.

The famous English navigator, Henry Hudson, sailed the Dutch ship, the Half Moon to the New World. He explored a large river in New York which was eventually named the Hudson River. Soon after, Dutch ships sailed to this newly explored area and called it the New Netherland. It was renamed New York by the English.

Wooden shoes clunked across the wooden sidewalks of a new Dutch-American city, New Amsterdam. Men strutted in plumed hats and women wore ornate dresses. Tulips were planted plentifully.

Two men wanted to expand New Amsterdam. They were William Usselinx and Peter Minuit. It was Minuit who bought Manhattan Island from the Indians for twenty-four dollars worth of trinkets. Manhattan Island eventually became part of the world's largest city, New York. Peter Stuyvesant, the last Dutch governor of New Netherland, surrendered to the English. They named the conquered land New York.

ENGLISH

PILGRIM HAT The Pilgrims were an English religious sect that settled in New England at Plymouth. Their black hats with gold buckles sparkled in the mid-day sun.

The English first came to America to set up new businesses. Since there was an abundance of wood and fur in America, it seemed like a good idea to come. What the English didn't know was that the land was inhabited by Indians.

A gentleman named Captain Smith was sent from England to explore the James River in Virginia. He set up the Jamestown Colony in 1607. Captain Smith was captured by a band of Indians. Pocahontas, a pretty Indian princess, persuaded her father to spare his life. She was successful and he returned to the colony.

English settlers continued to sail to America. Colonies were set up by the Pilgrims and the Puritans in New England. Who could forget the voyage of the Mayflower? English people settled in every state that the Appalachian Mountains run through. If you visit the states of the Thirteen Original Colonies you will see traces of the first English settlements.

FRENCH

FLEUR DE LIS This stylized iris is the traditional symbol of France. It stands for the patriotism of the French people.

Giovanni da Verrazano sailed to America in 1523 for France. He was trying to reach the East Indies. He failed and tried again many years later. Verrazano was unsuccessful, but he did explore the area that is known today as Montreal, New York Harbor, and the Carolinas.

French explorers sailed across the Great Lakes looking for the Northwest Passage, an inland water route to the Pacific Ocean, but stopped at the Mississippi River. It flowed south instead of west. The explorer, La Salle, traveled down the Mississippi to the Gulf of Mexico. At the mouth of the river he founded a famous city, New Orleans. He named the territory Louisiana for King Louis XIV.

There were many other French explorers who traveled as far west as Montana and the Rocky Mountains. They even traded with the Indians in New Mexico.

The French lost all of their territories in America during the French and Indian War.

GERMAN

SCHERENSCHNITTE TREE The German people are famous for their fine paper-cut craft work. The scherenschnitte, or scissor cut, tree shows their delicate work.

Germany played no part in the discovery of America. It is believed, however, that Leif Ericson, the Norwegian mariner and explorer, had a German sailor aboard his ship. His name was Tyrker. No one really knows if Leif Ericson really reached America first. It is a "possibility" just like Tyrker.

The Germans stayed home during the early years of discovery. German map-maker, Martin Waldseemueller, is thought to have invented the name America. He thought of it after reading the accounts of Americus Vespucius, an Italian navigator who visited the New World. The Germans made many fine maps for European explorers.

The ship Concord brought the first German families to America. Their leader was Francis Daniel Postorius. They founded Germantown in Pennsylvania. They came here because William Penn, the founder of Pennsylvania, maintained that his state would be a safe home for the poor and oppressed.

Most German immigrants settled in the states along the Atlantic coast. A famous German by the name of Sutter moved west. He found gold on his land and, thus, was indirectly responsible for people traveling west in search of it.

GREEK

KEY DESIGN The ancient design, sometimes called the Greek Key, was a very popular ornamental motif in Greece. It was carved on temples and buildings, and is used everywhere in the world.

Greeks started arriving in America just when gold was being panned in California. In 1848 one Greek immigrant arrived. He got rich and returned home. Most of the people in Greece who might have wanted to come to America were too poor to do so.

The biggest Greek migration took place at the turn of the century. The immigrants set up their own communities, mostly along the East Coast. Churches were erected and businesses begun. Many Greeks opened restaurants. The leader of an early Greek community was a priest who helped his people in any way he could.

Since Greece is almost surrounded by water and has a maritime tradition, many American Greeks earned their living as fishermen. Greeks fished for lobsters in Maine, for sponges and shrimp in Florida, and for all kinds of fish all along the coast. They helped supply America with netfulls of fish.

HAWAIIAN

PINEAPPLE The pineapple is the state fruit of the Hawaiian Islands. It is the sweet treat of this tropical land.

The original residents of the Hawaiian Islands were a mixture of Chinese, Japanese, and Filipinos. They all lived in harmony with one another. They were known as Kanakas and lived in grass huts and believed in many gods.

Things changed in Hawaii in 1778. This was the year that the first white man arrived. It was Captain John Cook. He tried to make friends with the natives but during a raid to recover a boat, he was stabbed to death. Nevertheless, the positive tales his crew told encouraged many other explorers to come to the islands.

Yankee traders and missionaries flocked to the Hawaiian Islands. The natives adopted European customs. Finally in 1894, Hawaii was annexed to the United States. Queen Liliuokalani lost her power to rule over the islands. The descendents of the royal family still have titles in Hawaii. The islands became the fiftieth state in 1960.

INDIAN (NORTH AMERICAN)

THUNDERBIRD This mightiest of Indian gods brought rain when it was needed. The thunderbird could turn the desert into farmland.

Columbus thought he had sailed to India. It is no news that he landed in the Caribbean. He called the people who greeted him Indians. What these and the other Indians of America didn't know was that from 1492 on they would see many "visitors."

It is very possible that the Indians were America's first immigrants. People think that the native Americans first came from Mongolia in Asia. The Indians have black hair, high cheek bones, and eyes with a slight slant just like certain Asian peoples.

There were hundreds of Indian tribes. The Seminoles of Florida, the Algonquins of New York, the Pueblos of New Mexico, and the Chinooks of Washington are just a few. Some Indians lived in tepees, huts, or pueblos, while others lived in cities built into the sides of canyons in the West. There were more than two-hundred different Indian languages and, of course, everything needed for life was handmade.

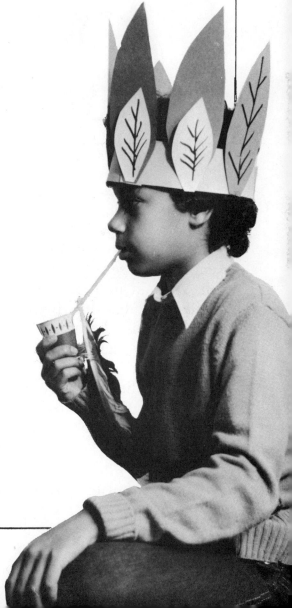

IRISH

SHAMROCK This three leaf clover is the floral symbol of Ireland. It is a good luck sign.

One hundred and twenty eager Irish settlers arrived in Virginia in 1620. They sailed on the ship Flying Harte. Most became farmers. They traded a field of heather for a meadow of golden wheat. It meant food on the table and money with which to buy pretty things.

The Irish weren't explorers but hard working people. Whenever a new frontier opened, they were there. Irish workers helped build the Erie Canal and many other artificial waterways. They enjoyed politics. One of America's famous leaders, Andrew Jackson, was the son of an Irish immigrant.

There is an Irish saying that on March 17—St. Patrick's Day—all the world is Irish. All you have to do to "be" Irish is wear something green and pin a big shamrock on your coat. It is as simple as that.

Irish immigrants brought many crafts with them to America. The Irish make the finest linens in the world. They crochet beautiful curtains and tablecloths. Then there is good Irish cooking. A real treat is a bowl of mulligan stew and a soda biscuit.

ITALIAN

TAMBOURINE Music and dance are important parts of the Italian heritage. The tambourine is used in the tarantella dance.

It was an Italian explorer, Christopher Columbus, who is said to have discovered America. His tiny ships didn't fall off the edge of the earth as those who thought the world was flat said they would. Columbus explored America and returned safely to Spain. Giovanni da Verrazano was the second Italian to arrive in America.

Both explorers sailed for other countries, Spain and France, not for Italy.

America owes its name to another Italian explorer, Americus Vespucius. He traveled all over Central and South America. He was one of the last Italian travelers to come to America until the late 1800's. There were, however, many craftsmen who did settle in the colonies. Their skills were needed.

Italians started arriving in America in great numbers at the turn of the century. Most found homes in the New York City area. They set up a "little Italy" with its own stores, and sidewalk pushcart fruit and vegetable vendors. The Italians were highly skilled at shoe repairing and hair cutting among other things.

JAPANESE

MOON FLOWER This flower is a popular motif in Japanese art. It is used in the Moni Kiri family crest.

The first Japanese people arrived in America by accident. There were many fishermen who lost their boats at sea. They either floated on a piece of wood or swam to a deserted island hoping to be rescued. Manjiro Nakahama was one of these fortunate castaways. He was taken aboard a whaler and brought to Massachusetts. He learned English and was given an English name, John Ming.

John Ming never became a citizen. He went home to his family. Another Japanese man did. Just like John Ming, Joseph Heco was rescued by the captain of a whaling ship. Joseph Heco settled in Baltimore and helped bring Japanese people to America.

Gold Hill in California was the first Japanese colony in America. Immigrants brought mulberry trees for silk farming, bamboo shoots for eating, tea seeds, and many other things. The colony didn't last. Most of the weary settlers went back to Japan, never to return again. Even though the first Japanese colony failed, Japanese immigrants continued to come to America. They settled on the West Coast since it was closest to Japan.

JEWISH

DREIDEL This is the top used in the game of lots played by Jewish children at Chanukah. It stands for the chances Jewish people have taken for a better life.

The Jewish people are the world's wandering citizens. They have moved frequently in their history, usually due to religious persecution. The first group of Jewish immigrants to come to America arrived by way of Brazil. Their first home was New Amsterdam. Peter Stuyvesant let them stay provided they would take care of their poor.

When the English captured New Amsterdam more Jewish people arrived. They came from Dutch, Polish, and Spanish cities. Most stayed in New York City. They set up their own communities and worshipped in synagogues. America was in many ways the land of freedom for the Jewish people.

Jewish immigrants continued to sail to America. They brought with them a few personal belongings and a wealth of traditions.

MEXICAN

PIÑATA The piñata is a decorated jar made of clay which is filled with gifts and candy and hung from the ceiling. Mexican children try to break the piñata. Piñatas are used for festive occasions.

Mexico was a land of Indian nations until the Spanish arrived. The Maya, Toltecs, Olmecs, and Aztecs were a few of the great tribes that lived south of the border. They built large stone cities and pyramids. Their land stretched beyond the Rio Grande into Texas.

The Mexican Indians were very peaceful. They did not remain this way for very long. Spanish explorers were in search of gold and jewels. The Indians didn't have guns or gunpowder. It was very easy for the Spanish to conquer them. The culture of Spain gradually replaced that of the Indians.

Part of Mexico used to extend into what is now Texas. Many Mexican-American wars took place for the land and eventually the Rio Grande became the border between Mexico and the United States. Many Mexicans stayed on the American side and became citizens. They became farmers and cattle ranchers.

Today most of the Mexican immigrants live in the Southwest. They celebrate fiestas, break piñatas, and enjoy singing and dancing.

NORWEGIAN

POPPY This flower is a popular floral design motif painted by Norwegians on wooden furniture and tin utensils. It is a sign of happiness.

The Norwegian settlers were a rugged and hearty group of people. The first group landed in Montreal and arrived in America in 1830. To get to America they hopped aboard ferries, trains, and even did some walking. Most Norwegians settled in Wisconsin, Minnesota, Iowa, and Illinois. The climate in those states was about the same as that of Norway.

In 1862 President Abraham Lincoln signed the Homestead Act. Because of it, a United States citizen could file a claim and receive one hundred and sixty acres of land. All he would have to do was live on the land for five years and it would be his. This encouraged many Norwegians to come to America and become citizens.

Norwegians became farmers and lumber jacks. Many worked in lumber mills and opened furniture stores. The women spent their hours rosemailing designs on pieces of furniture. Rosemailing is a folk art of Norway.

It was the steep, stoney, stumpy lands in Norway that made many Norwegians leave home. There was hardly room to grow enough food for a family. America provided for a better life.

PENNSYLVANIA DUTCH

HEX STAR The hex star is a sign of good luck. It is painted on signs which are placed on barns to keep away the evil spirits.

The Pennsylvania Dutch were not Dutch at all. It all started when German immigrants came to Pennsylvania. English officials would ask them what language they spoke. They would answer, "Deutsch," which means German. Since the word was difficult to understand it became confused with "Dutch." As a result, the new German settlers became known as the Dutch of Pennsylvania.

The Germans weren't the only group of people to settle in Pennsylvania. The Amish, Mennonites, Dutch Quakers, French Huguenots, and some Polish immigrants also settled in Lancaster County. All became known as Pennsylvania Dutch.

Most Pennsylvania Dutch people were very religious. Many were superstitious, and hex signs were made to keep away the evil spirits. The Pennsylvania Dutch 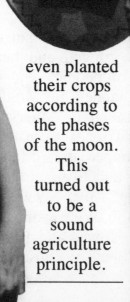 even planted their crops according to the phases of the moon. This turned out to be a sound agriculture principle.

POLISH

FIR TREE   The fir tree is a popular design in the Polish paper craft called wycinanki. It represents the tree of life.

A handful of industrious Polish settlers arrived in America in 1608. Almost immediately they built a glass factory. Since there were plenty of trees, they had enough fuel to fire the factory furnaces. Beautiful glassware was produced by this group of Polish people. It was sent to England and sold all over Europe.

This tiny settlement did not last very long. A band of Indians destroyed it. In a matter of minutes the factory became a pile of ashes. This event didn't stop Polish people from coming to America, however. Many went to live among the Germans in Pennsylvania.

The Revolutionary War entitled many Polish men to enlist and fight with the settlers. General Casimer Pulaski was one of the most famous heros of the war. He died valiantly in the struggle for the independence of a new nation. His birthday is now celebrated in all Polish communities in America.

43

SPANISH

PEINETA   This is a comb that is worn in the hair of Spanish women. It is an intricate and beautiful Spanish craft object.

Christopher Columbus's discovery of the New World encouraged many Spanish explorers to follow him. The first to sail to America was Juan Ponce de León. He came looking for the Fountain of Youth. Ponce de León landed in Florida and established the oldest city in America, St. Augustine.

Hernando De Soto was the next Spanish explorer. He marched through Texas and discovered Utah. De Soto claimed it all for Spain. He was followed by Fray Agustin Rodriguez and Juan de Onate. They explored New Mexico and tried to create a new Spain. They lost all their land to the Indians.

By 1860 the Spanish had conquered the Indians of Mexico and most of Central and South America. They were in search of gold and power which were not to be found in North America.

Spain influenced most of Central and South America and the islands of the Caribbean. The language, style of life, and architecture of these areas are Spanish-derived. Today these countries are independent. They had to struggle for their freedom from Spain just like America had to do from the British.

44

SWEDISH

RAM The ram in a circle is a traditional Swedish design motif usually made in straw. It is a popular decoration at Christmas.

The Swedes came from a wooded country. There were trees everywhere. They knew how to make a special type of wooden house. Instead of cutting trees into slabs, they made houses with logs. The Swedish people were the first people in America to build log cabins.

Delaware was the site of the first Swedish colony in America. The Swedes were proud of their new community. Unfortunately for them it didn't last very long. It seems that the Swedes raided a Dutch fort. Peter Stuyvesant sent soldiers to New Sweden. The Swedish people were outnumbered and surrendered the colony without firing a shot. All that remained was the first log cabin.

The next noteworthy Swedish immigration to America came two hundred years later. In the 1840's and 1850's Swedes came to America in large numbers. They followed the route taken by the Norwegians, and settled in the colder states. They were described as wild, rough, almost savage-looking men, with faces covered with grizzly beards. They were followed by able-bodied wives and healthy children.

UKRAINIAN-RUSSIAN

PSYANKA EGG The Ukrainian people paint eggs with intricate designs. These psyanka eggs are given as gifts as a sign of friendship.

Many Ukrainians entered the United States from the West. A priest from the city of Kiev was influential in making this happen. His name was Andreas Ahapius Honcharenko. He landed in Alaska in 1865, two years before William Seward purchased Alaska from Russia. Honcharenko found no difficulty living in Alaska. He became editor of the *Alaska Herald* and helped Ukrainians settle in America.

Small groups of Ukrainian people began arriving in America after 1867. Their first stop was usually either the Hawaiian Islands or Alaska. Just like many other groups of immigrants, Ukrainian people gave up everything they had to come to America. Some signed contracts without reading them. When they stepped off the boats, they found themselves virtually slaves on sugar plantations or in mining camps.

At the turn of the century, Ukrainians came to America in large numbers. The Russians who lived in Poland and the Ukraine also came. A Russian community was a hard working place.

AMERICAN

FLAG SHIELD This is the medallion worn patriotically by famous Americans. The stars and stripes symbolize America.

America is called the melting pot of all the cultures of the world. People came here for many reasons. Being free from poverty or from religious or political persecution were the most important. Most of the people who came brought nothing with them but their customs. The work was hard and long but it was frequently worth it. The immigrants helped lay the foundation for a great nation open to anybody in the world.

All of the groups that came to America brought their cultural heritages with them. An important part of a heritage is its arts and crafts. That is what this book is all about. Whether it is a Czechoslovakian handkerchief doll, a French silhouette, or a Pennsylvania Dutch hex sign, it is an important contribution. America is a living museum of ethnic art.

There are several crafts in this book that have no nationality. If you see the Flag Shield in front of a craft, it is American. It cannot be found in any other country in the whole world. It was made by immigrants in America. Since they came with very little, they had to make many things by hand. Using natural things, they invented many new crafts.

OTHER GROUPS

The world was different when Columbus sailed for America. Some countries had different names and others had no names at all. People came to America from every part of the world. When was the last time you met a person from Estonia, Latvia, or Montenegro? Maybe never, but handfuls of immigrants from these countries settled in America.

You have read about twenty-one large groups of immigrants who settled America. They weren't the only groups who came. When news of a new nation reached Europe, Asia, and Africa, people by the thousands set sail. The following are countries from which people came to America: Albania, Austria, Bulgaria, Denmark, Finland, Hungary, Lithuania, Portugal, Rumania, Switzerland, Turkey and Yugoslavia. Immigrants from "newly" formed countries, such as Australia, Canada, New Zealand, and the countries of Africa are also your neighbors.

An important part of the American culture comes from the small countries south of the United States. Columbus brought the Spanish influence to the Caribbean, Central and South America. People from Cuba, Puerto Rico, Haiti, Mexico, and several dozen other countries have added their names to the directory of American national minorities. Every group has contributed to this country even if their craft works are not represented in this book.

2

BEADS

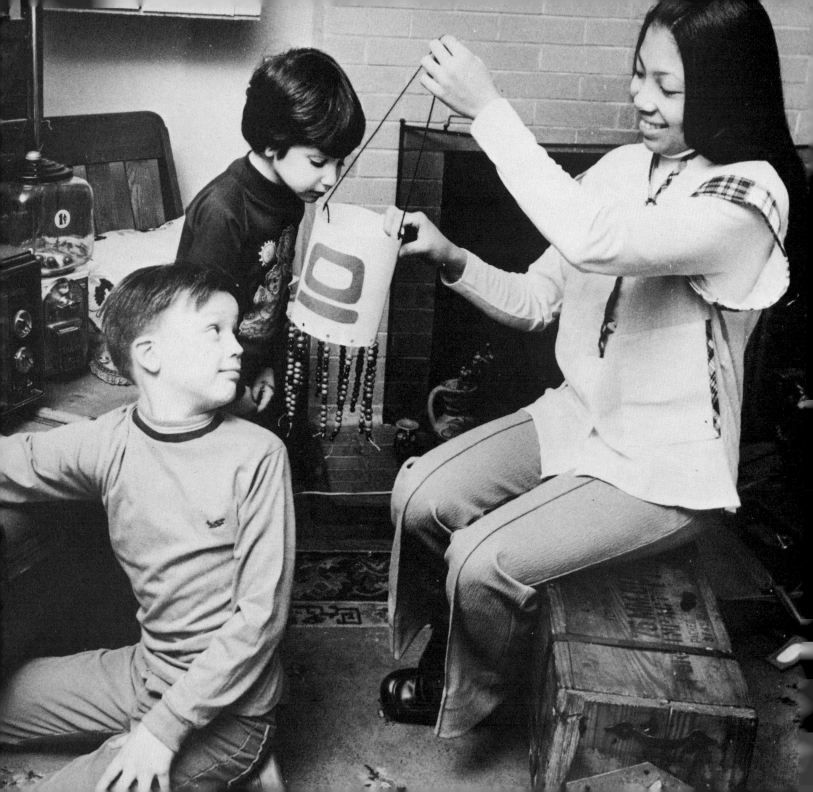

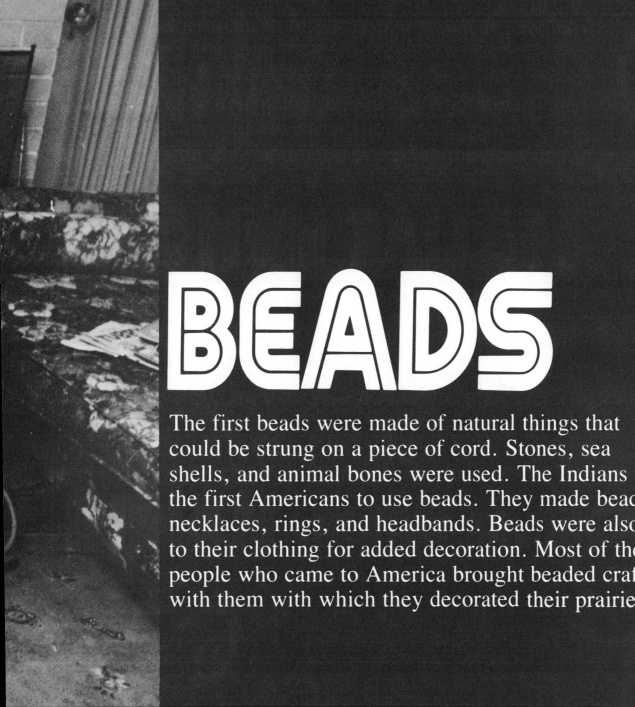

BEADS

The first beads were made of natural things that could be strung on a piece of cord. Stones, sea shells, and animal bones were used. The Indians were the first Americans to use beads. They made beaded necklaces, rings, and headbands. Beads were also sewn to their clothing for added decoration. Most of the people who came to America brought beaded craft objects with them with which they decorated their prairie homes.

DECORATIVE STUDDED

Most hand decorated dishes in Mexican homes are made of wood painted with gaily colored flowers. The immigrants who settled just above the Mexican border copied Mexican designs but used paint instead of beads. The finished product was a shimmering tray worthy of any kitchen in Mexico.

white paper plate
waxed paper
pencil
liquid white glue
small paper cup
paintbrush
seed beads

1. Choose a large, sturdy paper plate and place it on a sheet of waxed paper.
2. Draw a simple flower design in the center of the plate with a pencil. Add a wavy design around the rim.
3. Pour a little liquid white glue into a paper cup.
4. Paint a thick layer of white glue into the petals of the flower with a paintbrush, Fig. a.
5. Carefully drop colored beads onto the glued petals, Fig. b.
6. Glue beads to the center of the flower.
7. Paint glue over the wavy line, Fig. c.
8. Drop seed beads onto the glue.
9. Let the glue dry overnight.
10. Tilt the completed dish onto waxed paper to remove all beads that were not glued in place.

BEADED DISH

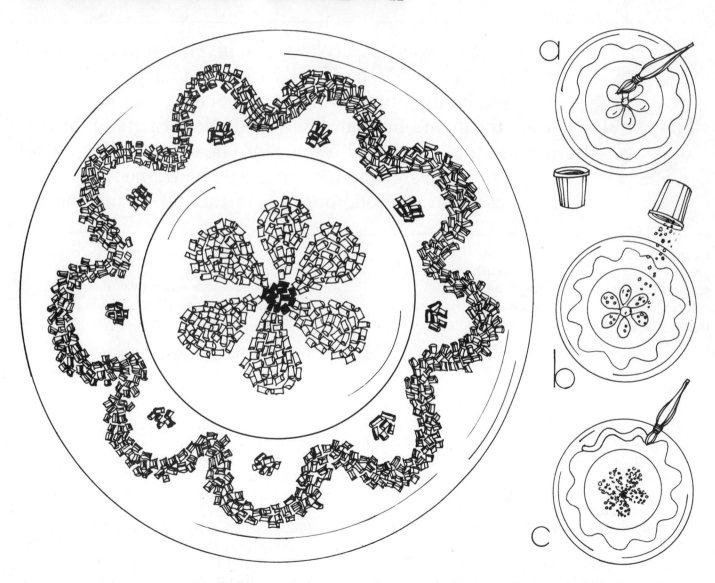

ROSE BORDERED

Photography was a relatively new invention in the middle 1800's. When a family saved enough money to have the family portraits taken, special frames were made for them. German families in New England turned wooden and cardboard frames into beaded wonders. They added floral designs to the corners. The framed pictures stood as proud portraits of the family members.

tracing paper
pencil
scissors
colored paper
liquid white glue

paper cup
paintbrush
tiny seed beads
lightweight cardboard
photograph or drawing

1. Trace the frame, the inside oval, and the roses from the book onto a sheet of tracing paper. Use a pencil.
2. Cut a piece of colored paper the same size as the frame in the drawing.
3. Transfer the tracing of the center oval and the roses onto the colored paper (see How to Transfer Patterns, page 20).
4. Cut out the center oval with a scissors.
5. Pour a little liquid white glue into a paper cup.
6. Paint in the small ovals of the rose designs with liquid white glue and a paintbrush, Fig. a.

7. Carefully drop seed beads of a single color onto the glued areas. Dry.
8. Brush glue onto the larger oval of the rose, and drop in different colored seed beads. Dry.
9. Continue gluing and beading the petals and leaves.
10. The colors for the roses are: brown for the small oval, red for the large oval, pink for the petals, and green for the leaves.
11. Let the frame dry overnight. Tilt the dried frame onto a sheet of paper to remove all the beads not glued down.
12. Cut a piece of cardboard the size of the frame for a picture backing.
13. Glue your favorite photograph or drawing to the center of the cardboard backing.
14. Place the beaded frame over the cardboard backing with the photo showing through the center oval, Fig. b.
15. Glue the frame and backing together.

KEEPSAKE MIRROR

APACHE BEADED

The Apache Nation spread out over an area that included parts of Mexico and the Southwestern part of the United States. Much of this area is desert. Beaded leather hunting bags were woven by Apaches for the braves. Most of the animals they hunted were small and could be tucked into such shoulder bags.

brown fabric or felt
scissors
tracing paper
pencil
carbon paper

needle and thread
beads
liquid white glue in an applicator-tip bottle
embroidery thread

1. Cut two pieces of brown fabric or felt a little larger than the size of this page.
2. Trace the arrow and tepee-in-the-square designs from the book onto a sheet of tracing paper with a pencil. (See Fig. a. for a picture of the whole traced design.)
3. Place the carbon side of a sheet of carbon paper over one piece of fabric.
4. Place the tracing over the carbon paper.
5. Draw over the lines of the tracing with a pencil. Push heavily on the pencil.
6. Remove the tracing and the carbon paper.
**7. Thread a needle with thread and knot one end.

8. Start beading the fabric by first pushing the needle and thread up through the end of a line.
9. Thread a bead and sew it to the fabric by pushing the needle back down through the line.
10. Bring the needle up through the line again, a tiny bit away from the last stitch.
11. In this manner sew beads onto all the lines, see illustration.
12. Fold the top edge of each piece of fabric back to form a hem. The fold of the beaded piece of fabric should go against the unbeaded side, Fig. a.
13. Glue the hems in place.
14. Place the two pieces of fabric together with the top hems inside, Fig. a.
**15. Thread a needle with embroidery thread. Sew the two pieces of fabric together around the sides and bottom, Fig. b.
16. Cut a long handle from felt.
17. Sew the handle to the sides of the bag, Fig. c.

56

HUNTING BAG

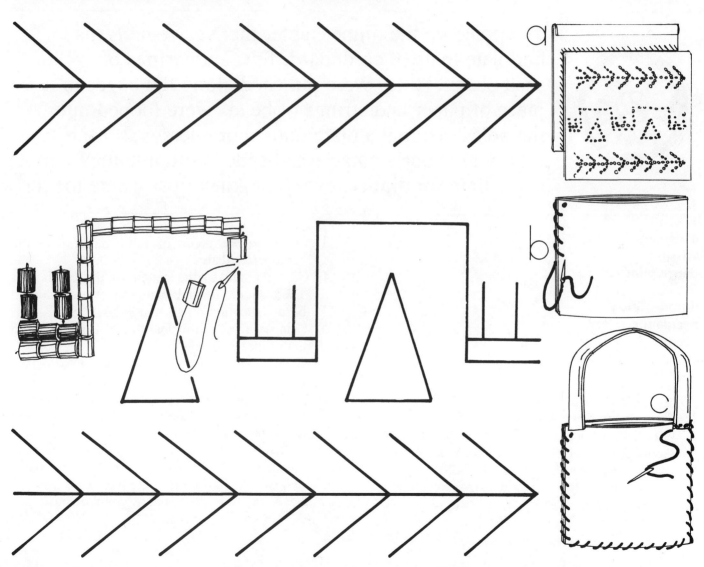

LOOPED FRINGE

To spruce up the dinner table, the Norwegians made hot plate mats of cardboard, felt, and strings of seed beads. Holes were punched along the edges of a piece of paper and strings of beads were looped into the holes. To make plate mats more personal, each family member's name was beaded onto a mat. When it came time for dinner, everyone knew just where to sit.

cardboard
scissors
paper puncher
felt
liquid white glue
needle threader
needle
embroidery thread
seed beads

1. Cut a square piece of cardboard.
2. With the puncher, punch groups of holes along the four sides. Start with one hole near a corner and make a few groups of two holes along a side, ending with one hole near the next corner, Fig. a.

3. Cut a square piece of felt smaller than the cardboard square.
4. Glue the felt to the center of the cardboard. There should be an equal amount of cardboard border showing on all four sides, Fig. b.
**5. Using a needle threader, thread a needle with embroidery thread.
6. String enough beads on the thread to form a nice sized loop, Fig. c.
7. Remove the needle from the thread.
8. Tie one end of the loop to a ''corner'' hole and the other end to the third hole in the same side as that hole, Fig. d. Trim away excess thread.
9. Thread more loops. Tie the next loop to the next empty hole and run it to the third hole from *it*.
10. Loop the entire plate mat as you did above.

HOT PLATE MAT

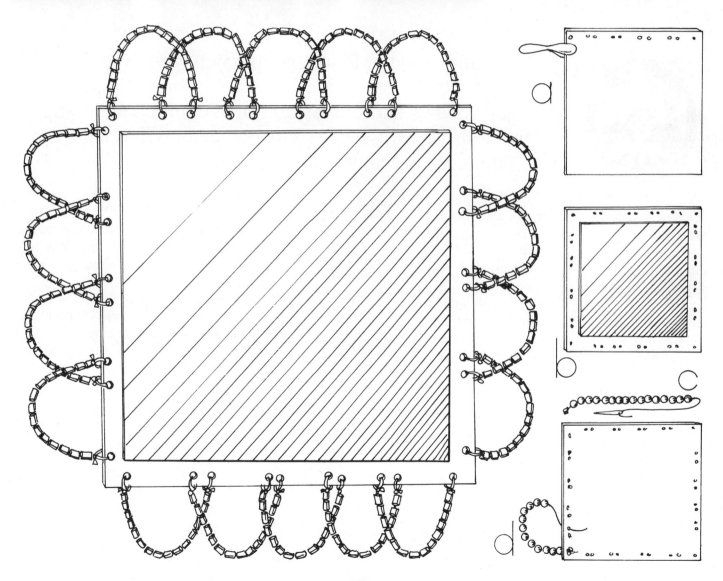

HAPPY TREE

Like all Indians, the Plains people believed in evil spirits. The tribe Medicine Man would brew up potions for sick squaws and braves, and made amulets to hang in the doorway of a tepee. The occupants of a tepee felt safe with an amulet to protect them.

tracing paper
pencil
scissors
cardboard
brown poster paint
paintbrush
needle threader

needle and thread
beads
yarn
paper puncher
colored paper
liquid white glue in an
   applicator-tip bottle

1. Trace the amulet design from the page onto a sheet of tracing paper.
2. Cut out the tracing and place it on a sheet of cardboard.
3. Trace around the amulet pattern.
4. Cut out the amulet from the cardboard with a scissors, and paint it with brown paper paint.
**5. Using a needle threader, thread a needle with a long length of thread and knot one end.
6. String beads on the thread to form a long length, Fig. a.

7. Remove the thread from the needle and tie the thread together, to make a bead loop, Fig. b.
8. Cut a small piece of yarn and tie it to the center of the loop, Fig. c.
9. Make two more bead loops as above.
10. Using the puncher, punch a hole into the top, bottom, and side corners of the amulet as shown in Fig. d.
11. Tie the ends of a loop into a side hole of the amulet, Fig. e. Tie the other two bead loops to the other side hole and the bottom hole.
12. Cut a cross from red paper, Fig. f, and glue it to the amulet, see illustration.
13. Squeeze glue dots around all sides of the amulet. Place a bead on each dot, Fig. g.
14. Place the amulet on a flat surface and let it dry overnight. In the morning tie a string to the top hole for hanging.

DOOR AMULET

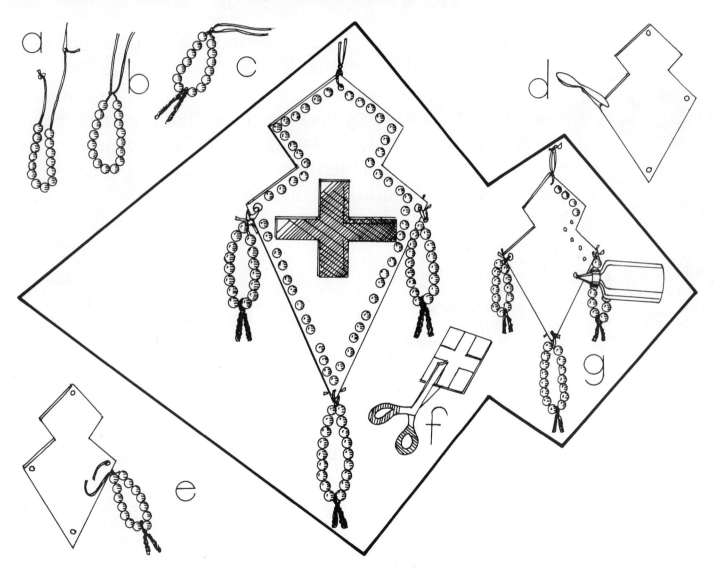

FESTIVE HANGING

A Japanese holiday is a celebration with music, parades, and beautiful decorations. Each special day has its own decorations. During the Tanabanta Festival, tall-as-trees lanterns are constructed and hung in the streets and buildings. In many Japanese homes in America, smaller Tanabanta lanterns with beaded fringe hang in hallways and dining rooms. You don't need a special occasion to make beautiful lanterns.

red and white paper
scissors
tape
liquid white glue
paper puncher
looseleaf paper

hole reinforcers
cord
needle threader
needle
embroidery thread
large beads

1. Cut a long, fairly wide strip out of white paper.
2. Roll the paper into a ring, Fig. a.
3. Tape the ends together, Fig. b.
4. Cut two letters just like the ones shown in the drawing from the red paper with a scissors.
5. Glue the letters to the front of the paper ring, Fig. c.
6. Using the puncher, punch holes along the bottom edge of the ring, Fig. d.
7. Punch two holes on the top of the ring, one opposite another, Fig. d.
8. Stick on looseleaf hole reinforcers over each hole.
9. Tie the ends of a long piece of cord to the top holes, Fig. e.
**10. Using a needle threader, thread a needle with a long piece of embroidery thread. Tie a knot at one end of the thread.
11. String large beads onto the thread.
12. Remove the needle and tie the unknotted end of the thread to a hole at the bottom of the ring, Fig. f.
13. Repeat the above procedure to make a beaded fringe for each hole. Tie one to each hole.
14. Hang the completed lantern by the top cord.

TANABANTA LANTERN

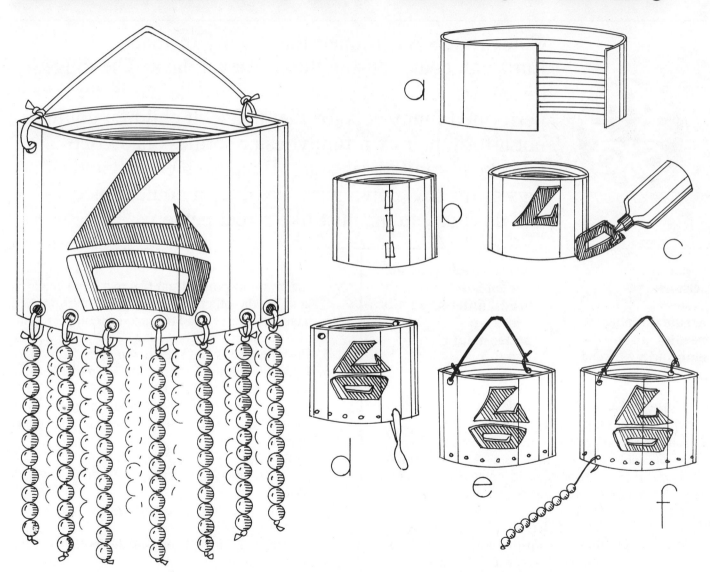

63

STAR AND BEAD

Court jesters entertained the royalty of many European courts during the medieval days. The king, queen, princes, and princesses sat while the jester performed funny acts for them. Czech children could not afford their own funny jester so they made one from beads and fabric stars. Because the arms and legs of the toy clown were flexible, it could dance and do funny things just like a real person.

paper or felt
scissors
tape
needle threader
needle
embroidery thread

**3 large beads or small foam balls
beads, different shapes and sizes
poster paint
paintbrush**

1. Cut a half circle from paper or felt and roll it into a cone, Fig. a. Tape in place.
2. Cut one large multi-pointed star, two medium-sized multi-pointed stars, and ten cross-stars from paper or felt. A multi-pointed star is cut from a circle and a cross-star is cut from a square, Fig. b.
**3. Using a needle threader, thread a needle with embroidery thread, loop the bottom end, and tie the loop into the thread with a big knot.
4. To make the jester's body, string the large multi-pointed star (1 in Fig. c.), a medium-sized, multi-pointed star (2), two large beads (3 and 4), the other medium-sized, multi-pointed star (5), a large bead (6), and the cone (7), onto the thread.
5. Push the beads and stars down onto the loop.
6. Make the arms by stringing a small bead, a cross-star, a long bead, another cross-star, and another long bead to a length of embroidery thread, Fig. d. Be sure to knot the end of the thread.
7. Make each leg in the same way as the arms with an extra bead and cross-star added to each thread.
8. Tie the arms to the body under the star collar, Fig. e.
9. Tie the legs to the loop at the bottom of the body, Fig. e.
10. Paint a face on the head bead with poster paints.

JUMPING JESTER

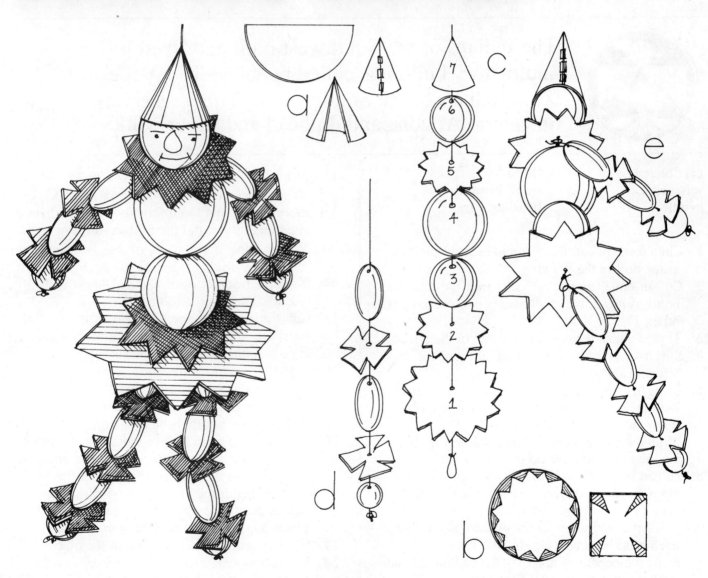

ZUNI HOOPED-SKIRT

The Indians of the Southwest built and lived in multi-story buildings called pueblos. Today the Zuni Indians of the Southwest live on a reservation in central Arizona and do bead and silver work.

cardboard **thread**
scissors **small beads**
needle **beading wire**

1. Cut a piece of cardboard about as wide and high as the doll in the drawing.
2. Cut an equal number of slits into the top and bottom ends of the cardboard very close to each other, Fig. a.
**3. Thread a needle and knot one end of the thread.
4. Slip the knot into the first slit on the top lefthand side of the cardboard.
5. Bring the thread down to the first slit on the bottom, over to the second slit, and then back up to the next slit at the top.
6. Wrap the entire loom in this fashion, Fig. b.
7. Tie the end of the thread to the last slit.
*8. Thread a needle, knot the thread, and string as many beads as there are spaces on your loom. (The figs. show only four beads.)
9. Place the beads behind the threads on the loom, each bead between two strands, Fig. c.
10. Bring the needle up and over the end thread and back through the beads, Figs. d and e.

11. String the thread with another row of beads— the number used for the first row, Fig. f.
12. Place behind the loom threads and sew them to the loom as you did the first strand, Fig. g.
13. Weave nine more rows of beads. Weave in three dark beads for a face, study Fig. h.
14. Knot the last row of beads to a side strand. Slip the weaving off the loom.
15. Cut the loops at the top and bottom of the weaving and tie every two threads together, Fig. h. Trim the ends of the strands.
16. Roll the bead weaving into a circle. Sew the sides together with thread or beading wire, Fig. i.
17. Make a hat just as you did the leaf in the Beaded Posies project in this chapter, Fig. j.
18. Make an arm from four or more beads threaded onto beading wire. Add another bead and push the wire into the top of this last bead. String another bead and bring the wire through the center bead a few times to keep the beads in place, Fig. k. Make another arm.
19. Wire or sew the arms and hat to the body.
20. String long lengths of wire with beads and twist them into loops. Add to the bottom of the body.

CHARM DOLL

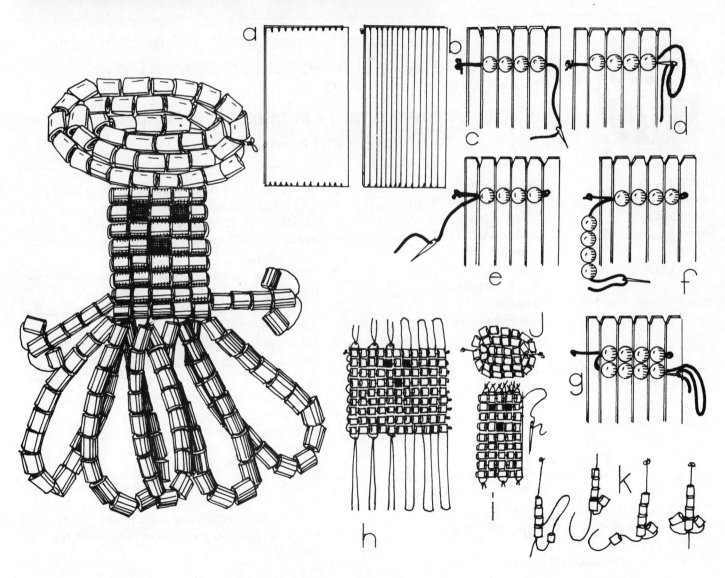

a
b
c
d
e
f
g
h
i
j
k

GOURD BODY

Gourds have such funny shapes that Czechoslovakian farmers turned them into comical creatures. They added arms and legs made from the beads of old necklaces. A painted face completed the bouncing bumpkins which were used as puppets.

gourd
butter
newspaper
paper paste or wheat
  paste
sharp knife
pencil
string
beads

paper clips
large beads or small
  foam balls
poster paints
paintbrush
tape
fine sandpaper
scissors
colored paper

1. Butter the outside of a small gourd, Fig. a.
2. Tear small strips out of newspaper.
3. Coat the strips with paper or previously mixed wheat paste.
4. Cover the gourd with overlapping strips, Fig. b. Add three more layers of newspaper strips.
5. Let the strips dry in a warm place.
**6. Cut into the dry paper strips as if you were cutting an apple in half, Fig. c. Cut into the paper around the gourd, from top to bottom.
7. Separate the paper halves, and remove the gourd, Fig. d.
8. With a sharpened pencil, twist a hole through the top and bottom of each paper strip half, Fig. e. The holes should be centered.
9. Tie a knot at the end of a piece of string and add beads to it, forming a short strand. Make three more strands.
10. Push the unknotted end of each strand into each hole, Fig. f.
11. Tie a paper clip to each unknotted end inside the paper halves, Fig. g.
12. Tie a paper clip to a piece of thread and string a large bead onto it as shown in Fig. h.
13. Push the paper halves together with the paper clip inside and the bead outside, Fig. i.
14. Tape the halves together, Fig. j.
15. Paste newspaper strips over the tape, Fig. k.
16. When the strips have dried, sand the entire body with fine sandpaper.
17. Paint the body white, and then add a red pointed design to the top and bottom.
18. Paint a face on the bead with poster paints.
19. String a colored paper cone hat onto the top thread.

CLOWN PUPPET

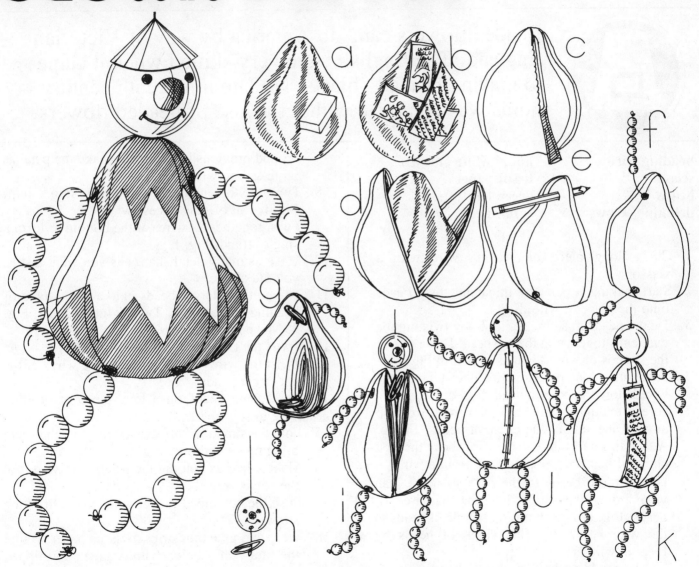

PICK-A-PECK OF

Beaded flowers came to America by way of Victorian England. The English were very skilled when it came to making beaded objects. No late nineteenth century home was complete without a vase of beaded flowers.

beading wire
scissors
beads
drinking straws

liquid white glue
tissue paper
green felt-tipped
marker

1. Cut a long piece of beading wire with a scissors.
2. Start making a petal by threading three beads onto the piece of wire, Fig. a.
3. Tie the beads in a circle, Fig. b. by twisting the wire ends together at the top bead. Bring one of the strands of wire down as shown in Fig. b.
4. Cut another long piece of wire. Twist it onto the wire below the bottom bead, Fig. c.
5. Thread enough beads onto this strand to wrap around one side of the circle of beads, Fig. c. Attach this half-circle to the wire above the first circle of beads by looping wire around wire.
6. Thread more beads to the wire so that it can wrap around the other side of the first circle of beads, Fig. d. Attach this half circle of beads to the wire below the first circle of beads by looping wire around wire.
7. Continue adding half circles of beads twisted

around previous half circles. Make the petal as large as you wish, Fig. e.
8. Twist the top end of the center wire into a loop, Fig. f. Cut off any excess wire.
9. Twist together all wires at the bottom to form a single strand, Fig. f.
10. Make as many petal shapes as you want just as you did above.
11. Thread three larger beads onto a long strand of beading wire, Fig. g. Twist it into a circle, Fig. h. Make another.
12. Twist the two circles of beads together.
13. Twist the wires of each petal to the wires of the six larger beads.
14. Thread ten beads on a long piece of beading wire to start the leaf, Fig. i.
15. Fold the strand in half, twist wires together, and bring one end down, Fig. j.
16. Make a leaf as you did the petals and twist it to the petals, Fig. k.
17. Push the combined flower wires into a drinking straw.
18. Wrap and glue thin strips of tissue paper around the straw and color with a green felt-tipped marker.

BEADED POSIES

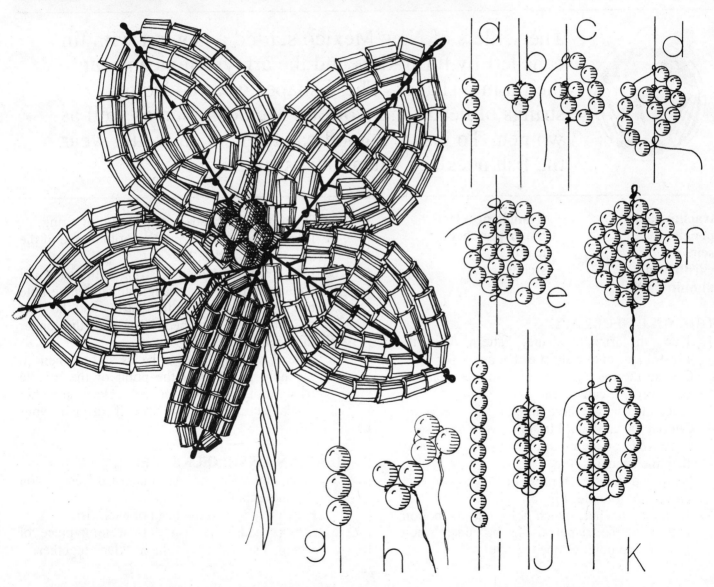

a

b

c

d

e

f

g

h

i

J

k

71

TIN AND BEAD

The settlers of New Mexico started a new art with tin cans left by fur traders and the army. Mexicans cut the tin into shapes. These shapes were added to strings of beads and worn by Mexican men as well as women. To insure a good catch, the men would wear the fish necklace when they went fishing.

tracing paper
pencil
scissors
cardboard
aluminum foil

triangle necklace
paper puncher
beads
string

TRIANGLE NECKLACE

1. Trace the triangle shape, Pattern A in the illustration, onto a sheet of tracing paper.
2. Cut out the tracing with a scissors and place it on a piece of cardboard.
3. Trace the triangle three times.
4. Cut out the cardboard triangles with a scissors.
5. Cut pieces of aluminum foil two times larger than the triangles, Fig. a.
6. Wrap and mold each piece of foil around each cardboard triangle, Fig. a.
7. With the puncher, punch holes into the bottom corners of the triangles, Fig. b. Punch a hole into the top point of one triangle.

8. Thread several beads onto a length of string.
9. Tie one end of the string to a hole in one of the two-hole triangles, Fig. c.
10. Thread another length of string with beads and connect it to the first triangle and the three-hole triangle. Finish with a third string and the final triangle. The more beads you use, the longer the necklace.
11. Thread two large special beads and tie them to the hole punched at the point of the middle triangle. Tie the ends of the necklace together (make sure, first, that it will fit over your head).

BEAD AND FISH NECKLACE

1. Trace and make the fish, Pattern B, just as you did the triangles.
2. Punch a hole into the head of each fish.
3. String beads and fish onto a long piece of string. Tie the ends of the necklace together.

NECKLACES

WORRY BEADS

Whenever something bothered a Greek person, he took out his worry beads and counted them in his hands behind his back, two by two. It proved to be very relaxing.

cardboard
scissors
yarn
thin cord
large beads

1. Cut a small rectangle from a piece of cardboard with a scissors.
2. Wrap yarn around the cardboard six times.
3. Tie the yarn at the top of the cardboard with a piece of cord, Fig. a.
4. Cut the yarn at the bottom of the cardboard, Fig. a.
5. Remove the yarn from the cardboard, Fig. b.
6. Tie the strands of yarn together a little down from the top knot, Fig. c. This forms a tassel.
7. Tie the tassel to the middle of a long length of cord, Fig. d.
8. Thread the two ends of the cord through a bead, Fig. e.
9. Thread fourteen beads on each end of the cord.
10. Tie the ends together leaving enough open space on the cord for the beads to move back and forth on it.

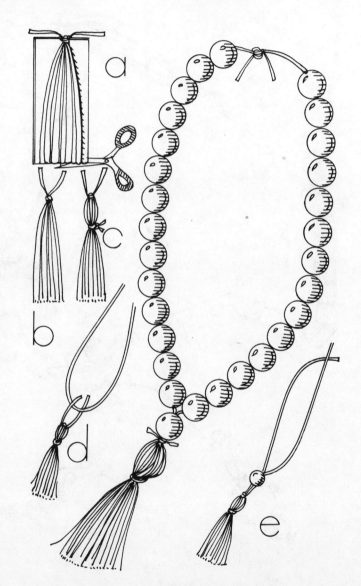

3

EGGS

EGGS

Besides being a breakfast treat, eggs make a great craft material. The shape and smoothness of an egg has inspired craftsmen all over the world. Many groups brought their egg crafts to America. The Ukrainians gave us the Pysanka Egg and the Polish their Wycinanki Pitcher Egg. Chicken farming became a booming American business and almost everyone could spare a few eggs for the dye-bath and paintbrush.

HOW TO BLOW

WHAT YOU SHOULD KNOW ABOUT EGGS

- When a project calls for an egg you can use either a blown egg or a hard-boiled egg. In some crafts a specific type of egg will be called for.
- If you are going to need a hard-boiled egg, have your Mom prepare it for you. Hard-boiled eggs should be boiled for at least seven minutes.
- Dyeing an egg can be tricky. A hard-boiled egg will sink quickly to the bottom of a glass filled with dye and may crack. The egg should be carefully placed in the dye with a spoon.
- To dye a blown egg successfully, you must allow the egg to fill with dye as you lower it into the glass. Unless you do, the egg will float on top of the dye.
- You can make dyes very strong or very weak. Add more or less dye—Easter egg, food or fabric coloring (see Things You'll Need For Each Chapter, page 16)—to a glass of water depending on how dark or light you want the dyed egg to be. Place dyed eggs on paper towels to dry. Work only with dry dyed eggs.
- Be careful not to handle eggs too much. The dye and painted designs can smudge and wear off.

HOW TO BLOW OUT AN EGG

straight pin
egg, at room temperature
bowl or dish

1. Twist a pin into the top or pointed end of an egg. Twist back and forth until you break through the shell, Fig. a.
2. Keep twisting the pin into the egg until you break through the membrane that lies just under the shell.
3. Remove the pin.
4. Make another hole by twisting the pin into the other end of the egg just as you did before, Fig. b.
5. Make this hole a little larger by carefully chipping away some of the shell with the tip of the pin, Fig. c.
6. Hold the egg over a bowl or dish, with the large hole down.
7. Blow through the small hole. The egg will flow slowly through the larger hole, Fig. d.
8. Rinse the egg under cold running water. Do not wash with soap.
9. Store blown eggs in a used egg carton. Do not use until thoroughly dry.

OUT AN EGG

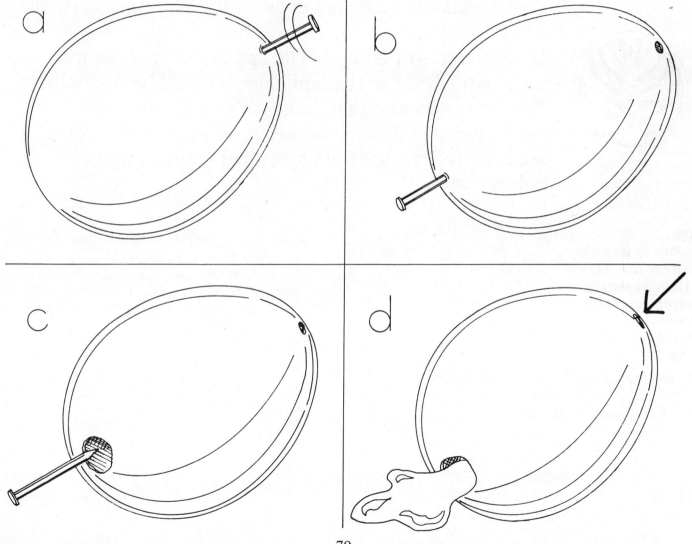

SNOW AND PINE

Polish craftsmen covered eggs with fine designs. They invented a tool that could spread a thin layer of wax on the surface of an egg. The egg could be dyed in parts in this way so that any design could be put on it. The Poles decorated their eggs with intricate snowflakes and spindly pine branches. Easter time was the occasion for this special egg embellishment in the Polish homes of America.

egg
yellow or pink crayon
red egg dye, food or
   fabric coloring
paper cups or glass
spoon
paper towel

1. Draw a line completely around the length of an egg with a yellow or pink crayon, Fig. a.
2. Draw a line around width, Fig. b.

3. Draw an X going through the point where the two lines cross on each side, Fig. c.
4. Draw shorter lines or branches coming from the sides of the X-lines, Fig. d.
5. Draw dots along both sides of the center lines, Fig. e.
6. Mix a strong batch of red egg dye, food or fabric coloring in a paper cup or glass. Dye the egg, keeping it in the dye for ten minutes.
7. Remove the egg from the dye with a spoon. Place it on a paper towel until it dries.

BRANCH STENCILED EGG

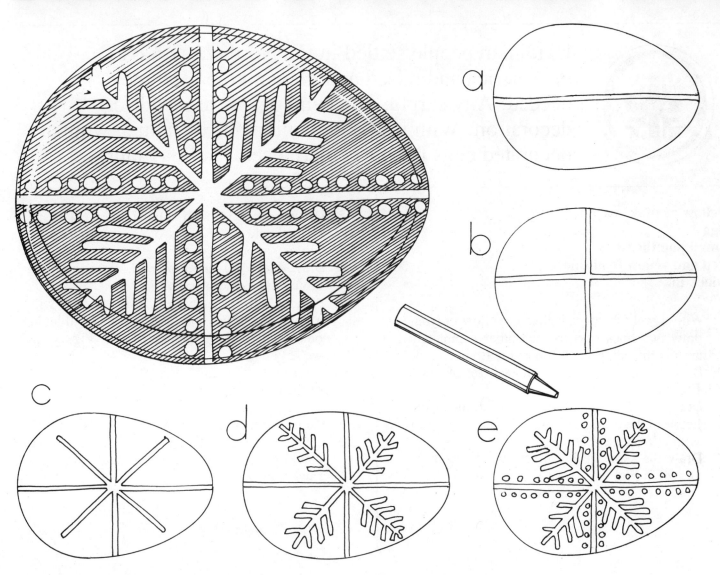

a

b

c

d

e

GEOMETRIC DESIGN

Ukrainian people settled in the Northwestern part of America and raised and grew all the food they needed. Any surplus chicken eggs were saved for decoration. With wax and paintbrush, Ukrainian women decorated eggs for the centerpiece of holiday tables.

yellow or pink crayon
egg
small paintbrushes
red and yellow food coloring
black ink

1. With a well sharpened pink or yellow crayon, draw two lines next to each other completely around the egg near its top and bottom, Fig. a.
2. Draw a zigzag line between each set of lines, Fig. b.
3. Draw two up and down lines in the space between the triangle borders. Connect the lines with a V-shape, Fig. c.
4. Draw the same design across the first one as shown in Fig. d.
5. Draw four lines, with smaller lines extending from them, at the sides of the center design, Fig. e.
6. Draw dots along the top and bottom lines and around the center design, Fig. f.
7. Paint in half of the triangles in the borders with a small paintbrush and food coloring. Fill in the outside part of the center design, Fig. g, as well.
8. Paint in the remaining triangles and the middle of the center design with yellow food coloring, Fig. h.
9. Paint the rest of the egg with black ink, Fig. i.
10. Let the egg dry. If some ink stays on the colored parts of the designs, scrape it away with your fingernail.

PYSANKA EGG

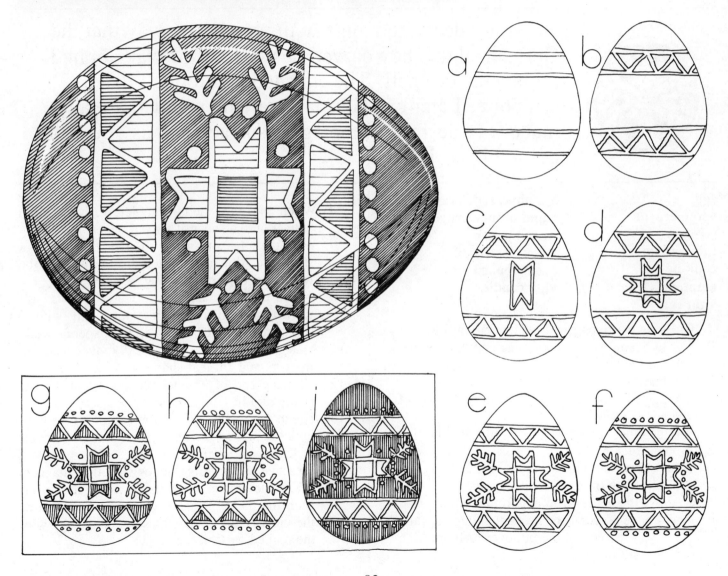

RIBBON WRAPPED

No group decorated eggs with wax in the way that the Germans did. They carved designs out of wax applied to the outside shell. The finished egg looked like a sculpture. Later on, German craftsmen added already made wax designs to the egg's surface just as you will do in this project.

egg
white crayon
scissors
thin ribbon
cooking pot
emptied, cleaned
 tin can

old pink, red, green
 and orange crayons
waxed paper
ruler or strip of
 cardboard
vigil candle

1. Color an entire egg with white crayon, Fig. a.
2. Cut two lengths of ribbon long enough to wrap around the length of the egg plus a little extra.
3. Tie one length of ribbon around the length of the egg. Tie the ends into a knot at the top of the egg, Fig. b.
4. Tie the other ribbon as above, opposite the first ribbon, Fig. b.
5. Add a small amount of water to a cooking pot and place the tin can into it, Fig. c.
6. Remove the paper wrapping from old pink, red, and orange crayons and drop them into the can.
**7. Have your Mom put the pot over medium-high heat on the stove.
**8. When the wax melts completely, have Mom pour it onto a sheet of waxed paper, Fig. d.
**9. With the edge of an old ruler or the side of a strip of cardboard, smooth out the wax on the waxed paper very thin, Fig. e.
10. When the wax hardens slightly but is still warm, cut flower shapes out of it with a scissors, Fig. f. Cut through the paper as well.
11. Melt green crayons as you did above, pour out the wax and cut leaf shapes from it.
**12 Melt the end of another old crayon above the flame of a lit vigil candle.
13. Touch the melted end of the crayon to the egg. Quickly press the waxed paper side of a flower or leaf shape over it, Fig. g.
14. Continue decorating the egg in this manner. Make the flower stem using a green crayon. Melt the paint of the crayon over the flame of the vigil candle. Draw the stem on the egg with the melted wax on the egg.

WAX FLOWER EGG

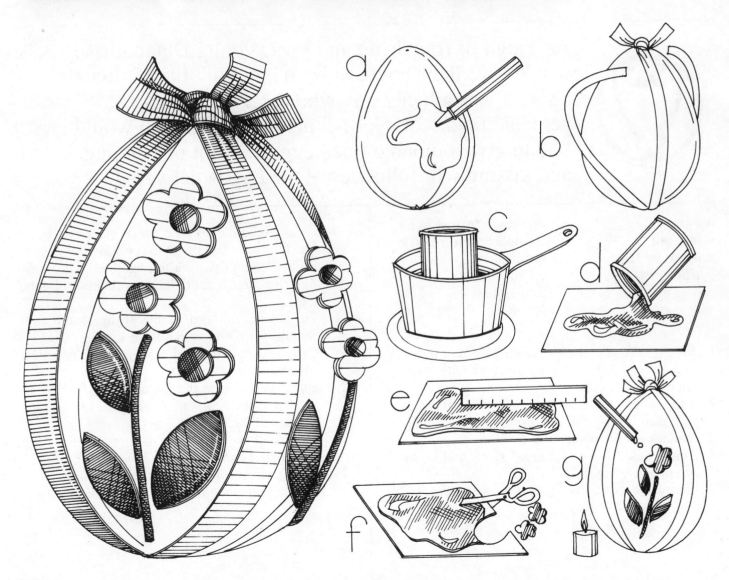

a

b

c

d

e

f

g

JEWELED, MONOGRAMED,

As a sign of friendship and love, young Dutch girls would give their boyfriends an egg with their initials on it. It was a lucky boy who received such a personal favor. Think of someone special you would like to give a monogramed egg to. A lot of hugging and kissing will follow once the egg is delivered.

blown egg
safety pin
crayons or felt-
    tipped markers

liquid white glue in an
    applicator-tip bottle
sequins
scissors
thin ribbon
string

***1. Enlarge the pinhole and larger hole in a blown egg by carefully chipping away the shell with an open safety pin.
2. Draw your initials on the egg with crayons or markers, Fig. a. If you use markers be extra careful not to smudge the drawing.
3. Draw pink flowers and green stems and leaves on the egg, Fig. a.
4. Squeeze dots of glue inside the letters, Fig. b.

5. Press a sequin onto each dot of glue, Fig. b.
6. Cur four long lengths of thin ribbon.
7. Feed a length of string through the holes in the egg. Be careful not to let the string fall into the egg.
8. Tie the bottom end of the string to the four lengths of ribbon with a loose knot.
9. Carefully pull the ribbons through the holes, Fig. b.
10. Untie the string at the top and pull the ribbons so that there is an equal length at the top and bottom of the egg.
11. Tie two of the ribbons at the bottom of the egg into a knot and then into a bow, Fig. c.
12. Do the same with the other two ribbons.
13. Tie the four ribbons at the top in the same way.

RIBBONED EGG

EGG AND FLOWER

Many traditions were brought to America when the first Spanish settlers built homes in the Southwest. Easter was a special holiday for them, and the centerpiece for their home dining table was often a cross made of blown eggs, field and cactus flowers. After the celebration, the cross was hung on the wall until the next religious occasion.

5 blown eggs   thin ribbon
safety pin   string
scissors   small plastic flowers

**1. Enlarge the pinhole and the larger hole of the blown eggs by carefully chipping away the shells with an open safety pin.
2. Cut four long lengths of thin ribbon.
3. Tie the ends of the ribbons together with a long length of string.
4. Feed the string through three blown eggs, end to end, Fig. a.
5. Slowly pull the string and ribbons through the eggs. Tie all of the stringless ribbon ends into a big knot, Fig. a.
6. Pull the knot up to the hole in the egg. Remove the string and tie the ribbons into a big knot against the other end egg, Fig. b.
7. Make a second knot, slightly above the first, in this strand, Fig. b.
8. Tie every two ribbon ends into a bow, Fig. c.
9. Tie a length of string to the ends of two short lengths of ribbon, and pull them through an egg. Do the same with the last egg.
10. Untie the strings and knot the ends of the ribbons on each egg, Fig. d.
11. Tie both eggs to the row of eggs between the middle and top egg, Fig. e.
12. Tie a ribbon to a small bunch of plastic flowers, Fig. f.
13. Tie the flowers to the center of the cross.
14. Hang the cross by the top bow.

EASTER CROSS

OCHTER-FOGGEL

One of the more humorous critters to come from the Pennsylvania Dutch Country is the Ochter-Foggel Bird. Brought to America by the Germans who settled in Pennsylvania, it was a sign of good luck if hung in a window or in a tree.

egg
safety pin
blue egg dye, food or
    fabric coloring
paper cup or glass
spoon
paper towel

scissors
white and orange paper
string
liquid white glue in an
    applicator-tip bottle
crayons or colored
    felt-tipped markers

**1. Before you blow out an egg, twist a safety pin into its top and bottom ends. Make two additional holes on opposite sides of the egg, centered between the two end holes, Fig. a.

2. Proceed to blow out the egg, (see page 78).

**3. Make all the holes in the egg larger by carefully chipping away the shell with the safety pin, Fig. b.

4. Pour light blue egg dye, food or fabric coloring into a paper cup or glass filled with water and dye the egg.

5. Remove the egg from the dye with a spoon and dry it on a paper towel.

6. Cut out three strips of white paper the size of the rectangle shown in heavy lines in the drawing.

7. Fold a little of one edge of one of the paper strips over and then back again, Fig. c.

8. Keep folding the strip back and forth, accordion fashion, until you reach the end of the paper. Fold the other paper strips in the same manner.

9. Tie the bottom end of each strip tightly with string, Fig. d.

10. Pinch the tied ends and push them into the three enlarged holes in the egg, Fig. e.

11. Squeeze glue around the folded paper strips in the holes. Let the glue dry.

12. Cut two small triangles from orange paper and glue them to the front of the egg for a beak, see illustration.

13. Draw an eye on both sides of the beak with a marker or crayon.

14. Tie a piece of string from wing to wing.

15. Tie a long length of string to the center of this string and hang the bird wherever you wish.

GOOD LUCK BIRD

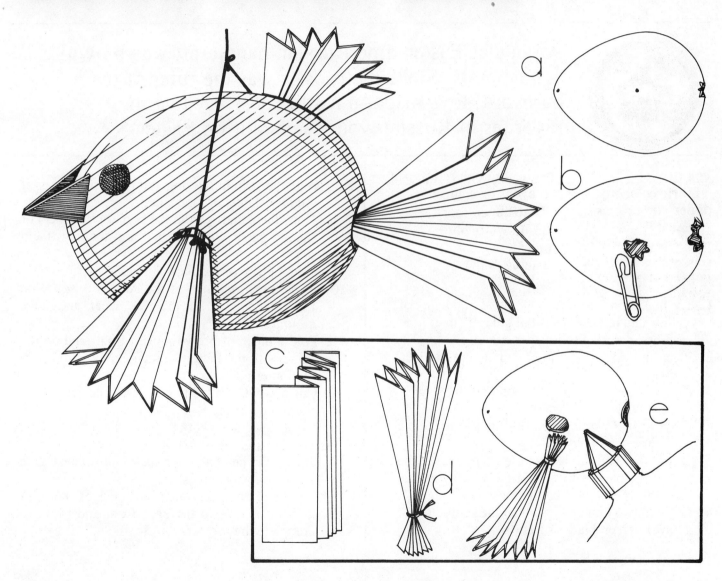

STRUTTING CRESTED

A popular Easter-time Russian handicraft was blown-egg animals. Since the rooster was the ruler of the barnyard, toys made in his likeness became the favorites of Russian youngsters during Easter.

egg dye, or
  fabric coloring
paper cup or glass
spoon
paper towel
scissors

white and colored paper
crayons or colored
  felt-tipped markers
liquid white glue
pencil
tracing paper

1. To make brown dye add equal amounts of yellow and red and a dash of blue egg dye, food or fabric coloring to a paper cup or glass.
2. Place the egg in the dye until it turns a deep brown.
3. Remove the egg with a spoon and dry it on a paper towel.
4. Cut a strip of white paper long enough to form a circular rest to hold the egg.
5. Draw two semi-circles next to each other at the top of the paper ring with a brown crayon, see drawing. These will be the rooster's "thighs."
6. Color in two orange legs under the semi-circles. Draw in green blades of grass.
7. Glue the strip into a ring and place the egg on it slightly slanted to one side.
8. Trace the patterns from the book onto a sheet of tracing paper with a pencil and then cut them out.
9. Fold a piece of red paper in half.
10. Place the dotted line of the Pattern A shape on the folded edge of the red paper and trace around it.
11. Fold a piece of brown paper in half and do the same with the Pattern B shape as you did with the Pattern A.
12. Cut out both traced patterns. Do not cut along the folded edge.
13. Draw designs on both sides of the head and tail as shown in the drawing.
14. Spread the head and tail apart and squeeze glue onto the inside edges.
15. Press one edge and then the other of the head and tail shapes to the egg, front and back, to complete the rooster.

EGG ROOSTER

DECORATED EGG

Polish people have perfected a craft of paper cutting and pasting that is called Wycinanki. It is a folk art from the farmlands of Poland. During the Easter season, designs of animals and flowers were cut out of paper and pasted on the walls of homes. Every year a new set of paper cutouts was made and the old ones taken down and pasted in the barn for the cows to enjoy. The egg pitcher was a popular egg-paper craft.

egg dye, food or
    fabric coloring
egg
spoon
paper towel

tracing paper
pencil
scissors
colored paper
liquid white glue

1. Add egg dye, food or fabric coloring to a paper cup or a glass of water and dye an egg.
2. Remove the egg with a spoon and dry it on a paper towel.
3. Trace Patterns A, B, C, and E from the book onto a sheet of tracing paper with a pencil. Trace Pattern D twice.
4. Cut out the tracings and trace around them on colored paper.
5. Cut out each shape. As you cut Pattern shapes A and B, be sure to cut into all short lines, Fig. a.

6. Roll the Pattern A shape into a circle and glue the ends together, Fig. b. This will be the base of the jug.
7. Push all the cut slits outward, Fig. c.
8. The Pattern B shape is the neck of the jug. Roll, glue, and flair out the slits in it as you did for the jug base.
9. The Pattern C shape is the spout of the jug. Fold it in half along the dotted line.
10. Glue the slits of the neck to the top of the egg and the slits of the base to the bottom, Fig. d.
11. Glue a colored paper band around the neck and the folded spout to the top neck edge, Fig. d.
12. Glue on a thin paper strip handle, one end onto the neck and the other at the base.
13. Glue the rooster, Pattern E shape, and the two flowers, Pattern D shapes to the egg. Add paper leaves, flower bulb, wing, and tail feather to the rooster and flowers.

WATER PITCHER

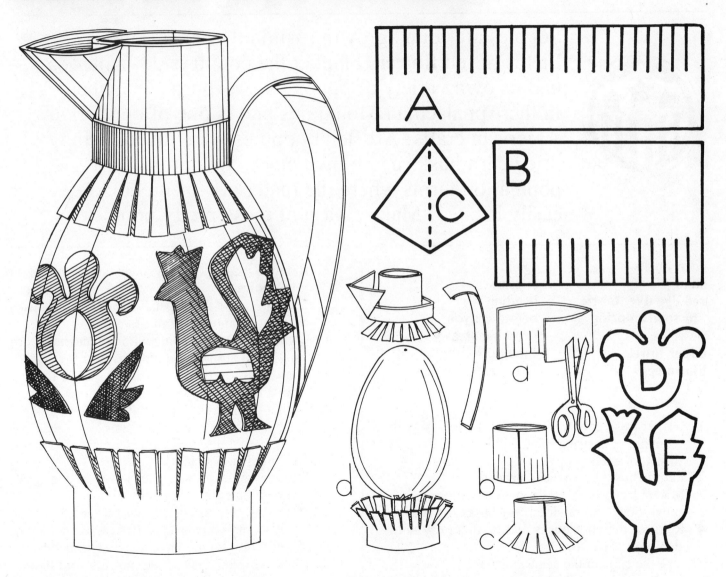

BOUQUET OF CORN

Poppies are found growing wild all over Europe. Fields of red flowers blanket the countryside. America had its own variety of poppy. It was born somewhere in the Appalachian Mountains and is one of our native American crafts. Artificial poppies were made, using dried corn husks and blown eggs. This project was popular on farms where the materials for it could be easily located. Make a vase of these pretty poppies.

corn husks
string
red egg dye, fabric
  or food coloring
bowl
paper towels
blown eggs

spoon
scissors
beading wire
brown crayon
drinking straws
safety pin
liquid white glue

1. Gather fresh corn husks and tie them loosely in a bundle with string. You will need about eight husks for each poppy.
2. Let the husks dry a week or more.
3. Mix red egg dye, fabric or food coloring in a bowl. Soak several dried corn husks in the dye.
4. Remove the corn husks and let them dry until damp on paper towels.
5. Dye the eggs in the same color dye.
6. Remove the eggs with a spoon and dry them on paper towels.
7. Cut long heart-shape petals from the corn husks while they are still damp, Fig. a.
8. Twist a piece of beading wire around each corn husk petal at the bottom point, Fig. b.
9. Draw dots on top of the narrow end of the egg with a brown crayon, Fig. c.
**10. Push a drinking straw completely into the large hole at the bottom of the egg, Fig. d. Chip away part of the shell with an open safety pin if the hole is too small.
11. Squeeze glue around the straw at the point where it enters the egg, Fig. d.
12. When the glue has dried, twist the wire of each petal to the straw just under the egg, Fig. e. Each poppy should have about eight petals.
13. Make a big bouquet of poppies for your home.

HUSK EGG-POPPIES

a

b

c

d

e

PRETTY TULIP EGGS

The German immigrants brought the egg tree to America. The tree is a symbol of life and the more tulip eggs on it, the better your life supposedly will be. If times were bad in the Old Country, the branches were bare. The only way your tree will be bare is if no one in your family eats eggs.

3 blown eggs
red and yellow crayons
drinking straws
safety pin
liquid white glue
cardboard paper
** towel tube**
brown poster paint
paintbrush
pencil
tracing paper
scissors
green paper

1. Draw two scalloped lines around each blown egg with a red crayon, dividing it into three parts, Fig. a. The lines should look like rows of little half circles.
2. Color in the end spaces of two eggs with a red crayon up to the scalloped lines, Fig. b.
3. Do the same with the other egg using the yellow crayon.
**4. Push a drinking straw completely into the large hole of each of the eggs as far as it will go. If the hole is too small carefully chip away some of the shell with an open safety pin.
5. Fix the straw so that it comes out of the egg straight.
6. Squeeze glue around the straw where it enters the egg, Fig. c.
7. Paint a cardboard paper towel tube with brown poster paint.
**8. Twist a sharpened pencil completely through the top side of the tube, Fig. d.
9. When the glue has dried, push the straw of each red tulip into the holes on the sides at an angle, Fig. e.
10. Put the straw of the yellow tulip into the top end of the tube, Fig. e.
11. Trace the leaf shape from the book onto a sheet of tracing paper with a pencil.
12. Cut out the tracing with a scissors and trace around it on green paper. Make two leaves.
13. Cut out the leaves and glue one on each straw of the yellow tulip eggs.

GROWING ON A TREE

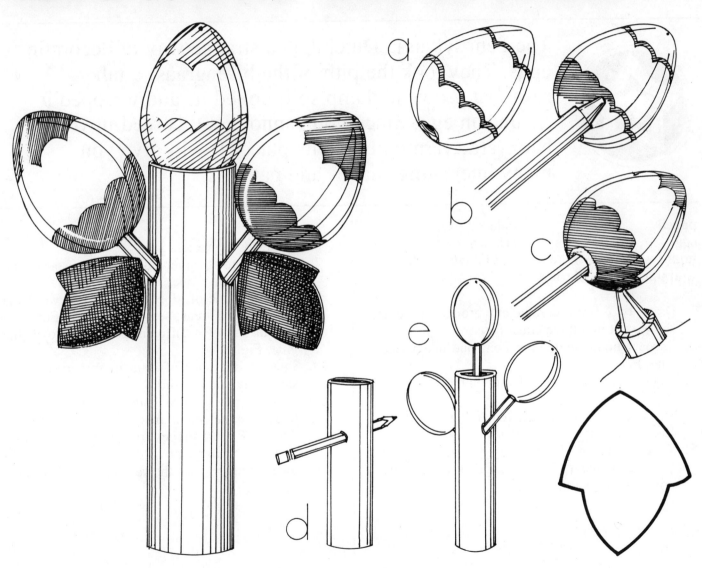

a

b

c

d

e

99

YARN WRAPPED

The Pennsylvania Dutch had a strange way of decorating eggs. They took the pith of the bisengraas, a tall rush that grows in damp soil, coiled it, and wrapped it around an egg. Since you cannot get this reed in your backyard, yarn will take its place. It will give you many interesting shapes and patterns.

pencil
egg
liquid white glue in an applicator-tip bottle

colored yarn
scissors
red fabric or felt

1. Draw two lines completely around an egg dividing it into three equal parts.
2. Squeeze liquid white glue along one side of one line, Fig. a.
3. Lay one end of a piece of yarn on the glue, Fig. b.
4. Squeeze more glue on the remaining part of the line and add more yarn, Fig. b.
5. Keep squeezing glue on the egg and laying on yarn until one end of the egg is completely covered with yarn, Fig. c.

6. Cut away any excess yarn.
7. Glue yarn to the other side of the egg starting on the other drawn line, Fig. c.
8. Squeeze a line of glue in the area between the two wrapped areas, see dotted line in Fig. c.
9. Lay an end of a different color yarn over the glue, Fig. d.
10. Squeeze out lines of glue in this area in the same way you just did.
11. Keep looping yarn back and forth over the glue lines until the center area is filled, Fig. d.
12. Cut small heart shapes from red fabric or felt. The fabric can be a red print.
13. Glue the hearts over the yarn in the center of the egg.

BISENGRAAS EGG

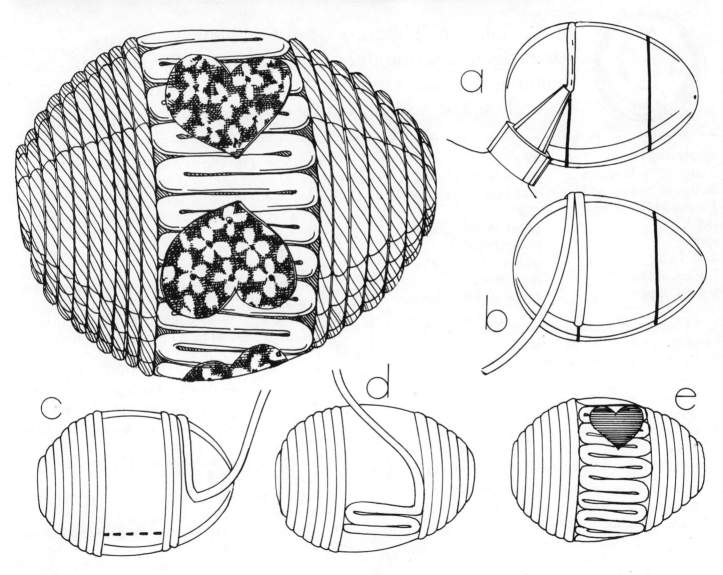

EGG TUCKED IN

In the Italian neighborhoods of Old New York City stores displayed dough baskets with eggs baked into them during Easter season. The basket was for decoration and also for eating.

measuring cup
2 cups of corn starch
4 cups of baking soda
2½ cups of cold water
small pot
spoon
dishcloth
rolling pin or can
waxed paper

knife
egg coloring, food
 or fabric dye
egg
paper cup or glass
paper towel
liquid white glue
paintbrush
round candy sprinkles

1. Measure out the corn starch, baking soda, and cold water into a small pot.
**2. Place the pot over medium heat on the stove. Stir the mixture with a spoon for four minutes.
3. Cover the pot with a damp dishcloth and let the mixture cool.
4. When dough is cool, remove it from the pot and place some of it between two sheets of waxed paper. Flatten it with a rolling pin or can, Fig. a.
**5. Remove the waxed paper. Cut an oval shape into the dough with a knife, Fig. b. Remove the excess dough around the oval.
6. Put some of the excess dough on another sheet of waxed paper. Roll this dough with the palms of your hands to form a rope.
7. Press the rope of dough onto the oval around the edge, Fig. c.
8. Mix egg coloring, food or fabric dye in a paper cup or glass and place an egg in it.
9. Remove the dyed egg with a spoon and dry it on a paper towel.
10. Press the egg into the dough oval so that it is a little closer to one end than the other, Fig. d.
11. Roll two more ropes of clay.
12. Place one over the middle of the egg and the other just below the first, Fig. e. Pinch away any excess dough. Push the ends onto the oval.
13. Make more dough ropes. Press them on a slant into the two ropes, Fig. f.
14. Roll a last rope of dough and place it across the slanted ropes, Fig. g.
15. Pour liquid white glue into a paper cup and brush it on all ropes.
16. Drop candy sprinkles over the glue and dry.

A DOUGH BASKET

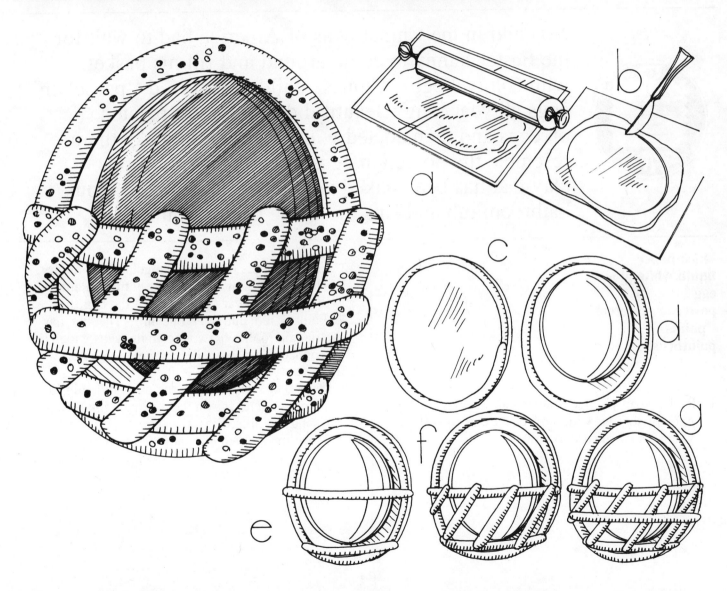

a

b

c

d

e

f

g

103

PAINTED "PORCELAIN"

No child in the Chinatowns of America had to wait for the Easter bunny to come around and fill his basket with colorful eggs. Chinese children enjoyed "porcelain" eggs all year long. Beautiful designs were painted on eggs and then coated with a varnish to make them resemble the porcelain eggs of China. Porcelain is clay that has been baked with a fine glaze on it. Your bathroom tub and sink are made of porcelain.

black paper
liquid white glue
egg
poster or watercolor
  paints
paintbrush

1. Roll a strip of black paper into a circle small enough for the wide end of an egg to rest in when it is formed into a ring.

2. Glue the ends of the strip together and let dry.
3. Hold the egg at the top and bottom. Paint two brown hills near the bottom of the egg, Fig. a.
4. Paint a red hut over one hill. The hut has a triangle roof over two rectangle walls which are connected by a smaller rectangle, Fig. b.
5. Paint a yellow sun over the hut, Fig. c.
6. Paint a brown tree over the other hill, Fig. d.
7. Paint green leaves on the tree and pink flowers around the hills, Fig. e.
8. Place the painted egg into the paper ring.

MANDARIN EGG

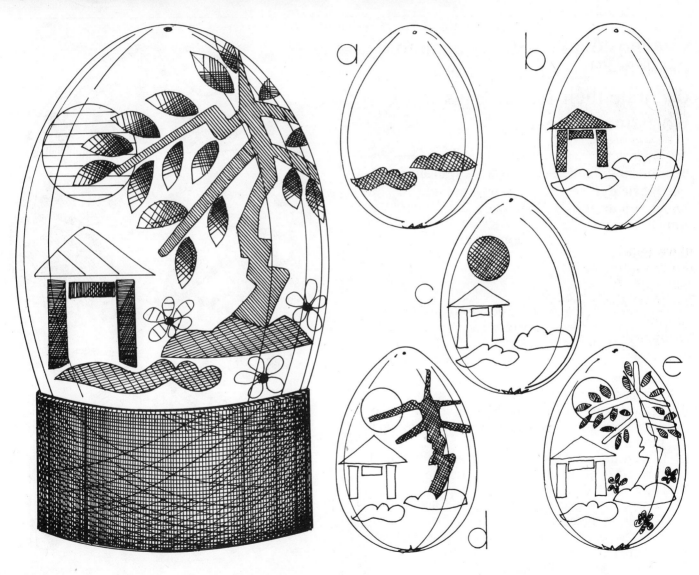

a

b

c

d

e

TEXTILE EGGERY

Czechoslovakian girls began to draw the designs that would decorate their Easter Eggs at Christmas time.

egg coloring, food
   or fabric dye
paper cup or glass
spoon
egg
paper towel

black, red, orange and
   brown crayons
scissors
orange paper
liquid white glue

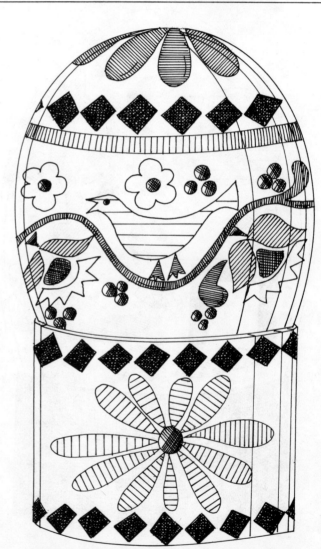

1. Add orange egg coloring, food or fabric dye to a paper cup or glass of water. Add an egg.
2. Remove the dyed egg with a spoon and place it on a paper towel to dry.
3. Draw a row of diamonds with a black crayon near the top of the egg. Add a red crayon border underneath them.
4. Draw designs of birds and flowers similar to the ones shown in the book. Use red, orange, and brown crayons.
5. Cut an orange paper strip long enough so that when it is rolled, an egg can rest on top of it.
6. Draw black diamonds along the top and bottom edges of the paper strip and a red and brown flower on the center.
7. Roll the paper strip into a ring and glue the ends together.
8. Place the egg on the paper ring.

4

FABRIC

FABRIC

Fabric was an important commodity to the American settlers and could not be wasted. Every snip and scrap was put to a good use. Torn clothing was repaired with patches. Quilts were made with patches and pieces of material became play dolls. You will be surprised to see how much creative fun you can have with your household's collection of scrap fabric.

HILLS AND DALES

Irish immigrants used worn-out clothing to make fabric paintings. Old clothing was cut up into squares or rectangular "canvases" and carefully cut fabric designs were pasted on. The creations were hung all over the home. Today, the Irish still create fabric paintings. Instead of using tweed to make the paintings, craftsmen now use felt.

small wooden picture
  frame (see below)
cardboard
scissors
blue fabric or
  felt
liquid white glue

paper cup
paintbrush
tracing paper
pencil
crayons or colored
  felt-tipped markers
colored felt or wool fabric

1. Have Mom or Dad find an old wooden picture frame that is about the size of this page.
**2. Cut a piece of cardboard that will fit into the frame.
3. Cut a piece of blue fabric or felt about the same size as the piece of cardboard.
4. Pour a little glue into a paper cup and, with a paintbrush, coat the cardboard with glue.
5. Lay the fabric on the glued cardboard. Rub the fabric flat with your hand.
6. With a pencil, trace all patterns from the scene in the book onto a sheet of tracing paper. The dotted lines indicate overlapping patterns.
7. Cut out each pattern from the tracing paper.
8. With a crayon or colored felt-tipped marker, trace around each pattern, transfering the designs onto pieces of colored felt.
9. Cut out each felt design piece.
10. Glue the scene onto the blue fabric as it appears in the drawing.
11. Frame the picture with the frame and hang.

FELT PAINTING

RAIN-IN-THE-FACE

Young America was in need of all kinds of people. Tinkers, tailors, blacksmiths, and even puppeteers arrived in large numbers. In the late nineteenth century the Lano family arrived from Italy. They were famous for their puppet shows. The Lano family created a new cast of characters for American audiences. Rain-In-The-Face was the popular Indian who could make it rain.

tracing paper
pencil
scissors
liquid glue in an applicator-
   tipped bottle
colored felt-tipped markers
brown and pink fabric or felt

1. With a pencil, trace puppet Patterns A, B, and C from the book onto a sheet of tracing paper. Don't bother to trace the features on the face, Pattern C.
2. Cut out the tracings with a scissors.
3. Place the puppet tracing, Pattern A in the book, on a piece of brown felt and trace around it with a colored felt-tipped marker. Trace another.
4. Cut out the two puppet shapes.
5. Trace two hand shapes, Pattern B, in the body,
and the face, Pattern C, on pink felt. Cut out the felt shapes with a scissors.
6. Glue a hand with the thumb facing up to each arm on one puppet shape, Fig. a.
7. Squeeze glue around the edge of the second puppet shape following the tiny dotted lines in Pattern A, Fig. b.
8. Place the unglued puppet shape over the glued shape, Fig. b.
9. When the glue has dried, cut slits into the sides of the body up to the glue to form a fringe, Fig. c. (the heavy dotted lines in Pattern A). Dotted lines in Fig. C show where the glue is.
10. Use a marker to draw eyes, nose, and mouth on the face as shown in the book. You can give on felt features if you desire.
11. Glue a felt headband above the face.
12. Put your hand into the puppet with your thumb and pinkie in the arms to make it work.

HAND PUPPET

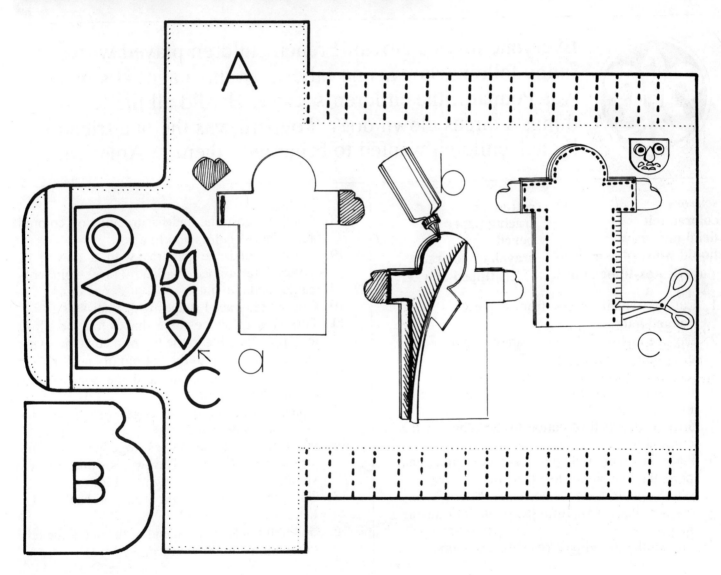

Everyone loves a clown. French children played with a funny fellow who was no taller than this page. His name was Poupard, the children's jester. He did all the funny things a circus clown does. Poupard was the one friend French children wanted to bring with them to America.

scissors
colored felt
drinking straw
liquid white glue in an applicator-tipped bottle
cotton
tracing paper
pencil
crayon or colored felt-tipped marker

1. Cut two small circles from a piece of skin-colored felt.
2. Lay the end of a drinking straw on top of one circle, Fig. a.
3. Squeeze glue around the edge of the circle, into the center of the circle, and all over the straw, Fig. b.
4. Stick a little ball of cotton to the center of the circle, Fig. c.
5. Place the other circle over the glued circle, and press the two circles together, Fig. d. Dry.
6. With a pencil, trace the costume, Pattern A, and the hat, Pattern B, from the book onto tracing paper.
7. Cut out the traced patterns with a scissors.

8. Place the costume and hat tracings on colored felt. Choose colors you like best.
9. Trace around the patterns with a crayon or colored felt-tipped marker. Trace eight costumes and two hats.
10. Cut out the traced shapes with a scissors.
11. Glue four of the costume shapes together, Fig. e. Apply the glue to the top of a costume shape and press the top to the bottom of another.
12. Glue the other four costume shapes together just as you did the first four.
13. Squeeze glue along the edges of one of the costume shape halves.
14. Press the costume halves together with the straw in the middle. The two costume shapes should cover the head slightly, Fig. f.
15. Glue the hat shapes to the front and back of the head, Fig. g.
16. Glue felt circles to each end of the hat. Glue felt eyes and mouth to the face.

JESTER-ON-A-STICK

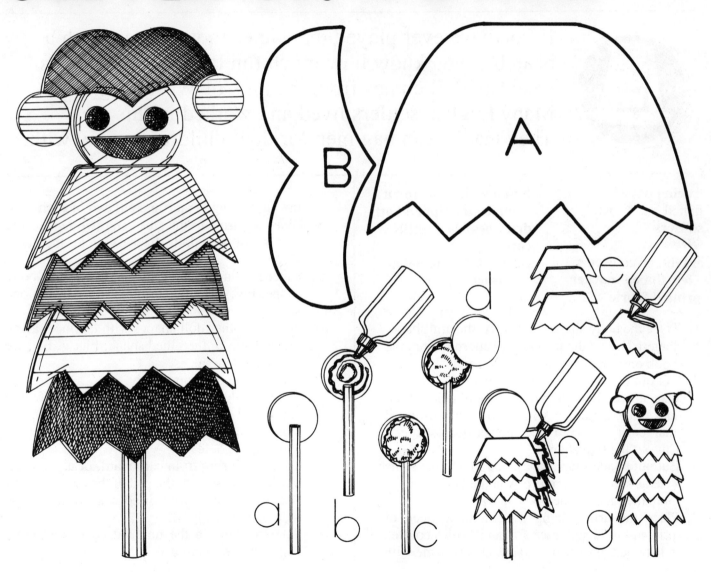

BEAN BAG

If you have ever played the game "hot potato" with a bean bag you know how much fun bean bags are. This bean bag doll comes from the hills of West Virginia. Many English settlers lived and worked in this area. They made bean bag men for their children to play with.

tracing paper
pencil
scissors
felt
crayon or colored
   felt-tipped marker
printed fabric

liquid white glue in an
   applicator-tipped bottle
dried beans or lentils
cord
cardboard or a metal
   washer

1. Trace the body shape, Pattern A, the arm shape, Pattern B, and the leg shape, Pattern C from the book onto tracing paper with a pencil.
2. Cut out the traced patterns with a scissors.
3. Place the body tracing on a piece of colored felt and trace around it with a colored felt-tipped marker or crayon. Trace another body shape.
4. Cut out the two shapes.
5. Cut out a face shape, eyes, and mouth the same size as shown on Pattern A in the book.
6. Glue the face to one body shape.
7. Place the arm tracing pattern on a piece of printed fabric and trace around it with a colored felt-tipped marker or crayon. Do the same with the leg tracing. Trace and cut two of each.
8. Glue two arms to the sides and two legs to the bottom of the doll shape without the face, Fig. a.
9. Squeeze glue around the edge of this body shape, Fig. b. Leave a little of the edge on one side (see arrow in illustration) unglued.
10. Place the other doll shape, with the face facing you, on top of the glued shape, Fig. c. Be sure the edges line up.
11. Let the glue dry completely.
12. Twist a hole through the top of the doll with a sharpened pencil.
13. Tie a length of cord to the top of the doll through the hole.
14. Cut a small ring from cardboard, or use a metal washer, and tie it to the end of the cord, Fig. c.
15. Half fill the doll with dried beans through the side opening, Fig. d.
16. Squeeze glue on the unglued edges and press together. Let them dry.

TOSS-AND-CATCH MAN

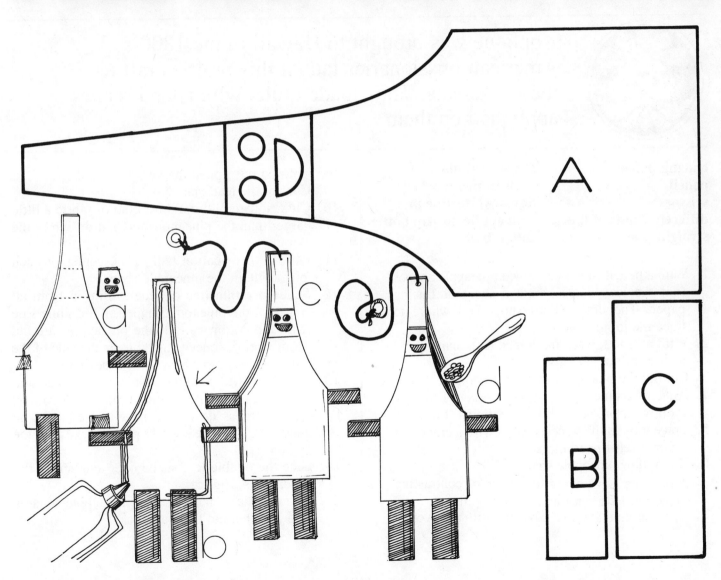

ISLAND APPLIQUÉD

Appliqué was brought to Hawaii in the 1800's. American missionaries taught this prairie craft to the Hawaiians. They made quilts with island scenes appliquéd on them.

tracing paper
pencil
scissors
different kinds of fabric
straight pins

crayon or colored
   felt-tipped marker
liquid white glue in
   an applicator-tip bottle
cotton balls

1. With a pencil, trace the joined pineapple shapes (not the leaf shapes) onto a sheet of tracing paper. The dotted lines show you where to trace the joining bar.
2. With a pencil, trace the joined leaf shapes onto a sheet of tracing paper.
3. Cut out the pineapple and leaf tracings.
**4. Attach the pineapple tracing to a piece of fabric (yellow or orange) with straight pins, Fig. a.
5. Trace around the traced pattern with a crayon or colored felt-tipped marker.
6. Cut out the pineapple shape.
**7. Attach the leaf tracing to a piece of contrasting color fabric (green) with straight pins.
8. Trace around the traced pattern with a crayon or colored felt-tipped marker.
9. Cut out the leaf shape.
10. Cut a square out of a third kind of fabric a little larger than the pineapple and leaf design in the book.
11. Glue a small cotton ball to the center of each pineapple in the pineapple shape.
12. Squeeze a thin line of glue a little in from all edges of the pineapple shape, on the same side with the cotton ball. If the pineapples are cut from a print, squeeze the glue on the side of the fabric that doesn't have a clear design.
13. Carefully lift up the glued pineapple piece and place it on the fabric square, corner to corner, Fig. b. Press down all the glued edges. The pineapples will be slightly puffy because of the cotton.
14. Glue the double leaf shape over and across the pineapples, Fig. c.
15. You can make many of these pineapple squares and join them to form a quilt.

PINEAPPLE QUILT

CANTONESE DESIGN

If you like to go fishing, you know how important a landing net can be. The Chinese frequently used net as a backing for appliqué designs. Shapes were cut from fabric and sewn to the net background. The completed appliqué design was hung in the home or sold in stores.

tracing paper
pencil
scissors
fabric or felt
straight pins

crayons or colored
   felt-tipped markers
netting
waxed paper
liquid white glue in
   applicator-tipped bottle

1. With a pencil, trace all of the pattern parts of the design in the book onto a sheet of tracing paper. The part of the table covered by the body shape is drawn in dotted lines.
2. Cut out the patterns from the tracing paper with a scissors.

**3. Attach the traced patterns on pieces of scrap fabric or felt with straight pins. Trace around each pattern with a crayon or marker, Fig. a.
4. Cut the drawn patterns from the fabric.
5. Cut a piece of netting about the size of this page. (If you do not know what netting is, see Things You'll Need on page 17.)
6. Place the netting on a piece of waxed paper.
7. Squeeze glue on the backside of each piece of the design, a little in from the edges, Fig. b.
8. Place the glued sides of each glued piece on the net in the same arrangement as shown in the book. Allow to dry.

APPLIQUÉD ON NET

TWO GATHERED

The trek across the plains was long and tiresome. The handkerchief doll gave the children of adventurous settlers hours of companionship. The two dolls in this project are very simple to make. The Rolled Doll is American and the Stuffed Head Doll came from Czechoslovakia. Both can be carried in a pocket and will keep you company on long trips with Mom and Dad.

two handkerchiefs
cotton
ribbon
colored felt-tipped markers
string

STUFFED HEAD DOLL

1. Place a ball of cotton in the center of an opened handkerchief, Fig. a.
2. Bring the sides over the cotton, Fig. b.
3. Tie the folded handkerchief together under the cotton ball with a length of ribbon to form a head, Fig. c.
4. Draw a face on the head with colored felt-tipped markers.

ROLLED LEGS DOLL

1. Place an opened handkerchief on a table with a point at the top and bottom, Fig. d.

2. Bring the bottom point up to the top point, Fig. e.
3. Start rolling one corner, Fig. f.
4. Roll the corner at an angle until you are very close to the top point, Figs. g and h.
5. Roll the opposite corner the same way as above, Fig. i.
6. Carefully turn the rolled handkerchief over, Fig. j.
7. Cut a small circle from a light colored fabric and place a ball of cotton on it, Fig. k.
8. Bring the circle over the cotton ball. Tie the circle under the cotton ball with string, Fig. k., as you did in the Stuffed Head Doll.
9. Draw a face on the tied cotton head with colored felt-tipped markers.
10. Place the face on the rolled handkerchief a little down from the top point, Fig. l.
11. Fold both sides of the rolled handkerchief over the tied end of the face. Tie the handkerchief together with ribbon, Fig. m.

HANDKERCHIEF DOLLS

BLUE RIDGE MOUNTAIN

Many communities of English settlers made their homes in the Blue Ridge Mountains of Virginia. After a hard day's work in the fields, craftwork was a pleasurable activity. The roll doll was a favorite project that was fun and easy to make.

colored and print fabric   small safety pins
scissors   colored felt-tipped
liquid white glue in   markers
   an applicator-tip bottle   yarn

1. Cut a very long rectangular piece of fabric. It should be as high as the doll in the drawing.
2. Roll one short end of the fabric into a very tight roll, Fig. a.
3. Squeeze glue along the opposite end, Fig. b, and press it to the roll, Fig. c.
4. Cut a square the size of the open arms in the drawing from another piece of fabric.
5. Roll and glue the square as you did above, Figs. d, e, and f.
**6. Pin the small roll across the large roll a little down from the top with small safety pins, Fig. g. The glued sides of both rolls should face you. This is the back of the doll.
7. Draw a face on the front of the doll with colored felt-tipped markers.
8. Gather long lengths of yarn at their centers and tie together with a small piece of yarn, Fig. h.

9. Glue the center of the tied yarn to the top front of the large roll. Bring the hanging yarn to the back, Fig. i.
10. Gather the yarn at the back and make a braid, Fig. j. (See Fluffy Pom-Pom Donkey Pull, on page 234 for braiding instructions.) Tie the end of the braid with a piece of yarn.
11. Cut a piece of printed fabric as high as the distance between the bottom of the large roll and the arms.
12. Wrap the fabric around the bottom of the doll and glue it to the back for the skirt, Fig. k.
13. Cut a piece of fabric that is as long as the distance between the top of the head and the bottom of the skirt. It should be slightly smaller in width than the outstretched arms.
14. Cut a hole in the center of this fabric large enough to fit over the head, Cut a point into one end of the hole, Fig. 1.
15. Slip the fabric over the head with the point in front, Fig. m.
16. Cut a long skinny piece of printed fabric and tie it around the fabric blouse to make a waist, Fig. m.

ROLL DOLL

FESTIVAL OF LOTS

The Jewish people brought much of their culture with them to America. One favorite Jewish festival is Purim, known as the Festival of Lots. Children are told of the story of Purim by puppets much like the ones you will make in this project.

colored felt rectangles
scissors
liquid white glue
sharpened pencil
cord

1. Roll six felt rectangles into cylinders and glue the ends together, Fig. a.
2. Study the drawing carefully. The puppets are:
   PUPPET 1—King Ahasuerus
   PUPPET 2—Queen Esther
   PUPPET 3—Mordecai, the good minister
   PUPPET 4—Haman, the wicked minister
   PUPPET 5—The Servant
   PUPPET 6—The Horse
3. Glue a strip of felt around all the dolls except one, the horse, for the hair, Fig. b.
4. Glue a square of felt to the strips of hair for a face, Fig. c.
5. Cut facial features for each puppet from pieces of scrap felt. Glue them to each face, Fig. d. See the illustration for the horse's features.
6. Glue on felt crowns, hats, and costumes to each puppet, Fig. d. Make the horse's mane from strips of felt glued along one side starting at the top.
7. Cut two felt arms, see drawings, for each puppet. Glue the edge of the arm to the body so the arms will stick out, Fig. e.
8. Make two holes in the top of each puppet with the point of a sharpened pencil. The holes should be opposite each other on both sides of the head.
9. Tie a piece of cord through the two holes of each puppet. Tie a longer length of cord to the center of the tied cord, Fig. f.
10. Dangle the puppets on a puppet stage by the strings.

PURIM PUPPETS

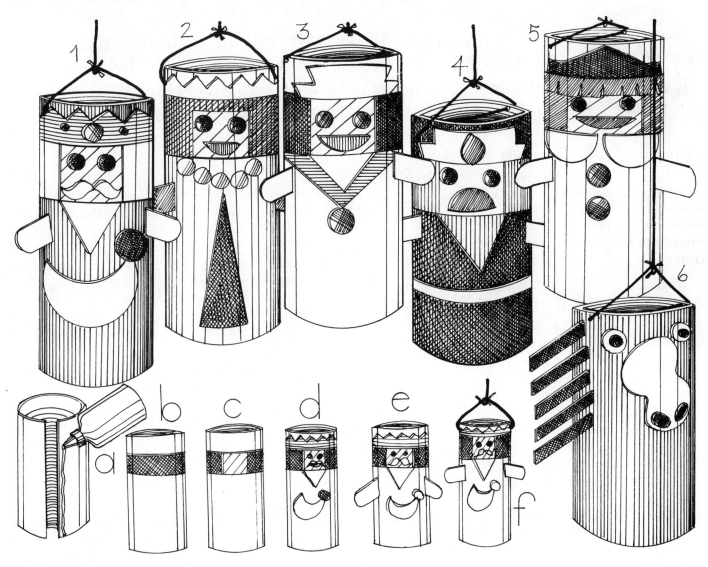

PATCHWORK SKIRT

Pioneer women as well as Seminole Indians also knew about patchwork. In their warm Florida homes they added patchwork designs to their clothing. They made dolls from palmetto bark with patchwork costumes. Their young papooses loved their doll playmates.

tracing paper
pencil
scissors
brown felt
crayon or colored
  felt-tipped marker
cotton

liquid white glue in
  an applicator-tip bottle
scrap fabric
cord
rickrack
seed beads
string

1. With a pencil, trace the doll shape, Pattern A, and the hat, Pattern B (inside the doll shape) from the book onto a sheet of tracing paper.
2. Cut out the doll and hat tracing with a scissors.
3. Place the doll tracing on brown felt. Trace around it and cut out two.
4. Place cotton on one doll shape, Fig. a. Keep the cotton away from the edges of the doll shape.
5. Squeeze glue around all edges of the doll shape that has the cotton on it, Fig. b.
6. Place the other doll shape over the glued shape. Press the edges of both shapes together. Let the doll dry.
7. Cut a long piece of fabric as wide as the distance from the neck of the doll to the bottom edge.
8. Cut small squares of scrap fabric all the same size. Use different colors.
9. Glue the squares along the bottom edge of the long piece of fabric, Fig. c.
10. Cut a length of cord longer than the fabric.
11. Turn the fabric over, and squeeze glue along the top edge.
12. Place the cord a little down from the glued edge. Fold the edge over the cord, Fig. d. The cord should move freely. Let dry.
13. Fold the fabric over with the squares inside, Fig. e. Glue the sides of the fabric together. This is the doll's skirt.
14. Make a smaller skirt just as you made the large skirt. Glue rickrack to the bottom edge of this skirt, Fig. f.
15. When both skirts have dried, turn them inside out. Fit the large skirt over the doll and tie its cord around the neck, Fig. g. Do the same with the smaller skirt, Fig. h.
16. Trace the hat pattern onto cardboard and cut out.
17. Color the hat with a black felt-tipped marker or crayon and glue it to the head. Add a string of seed beads around the neck, and glue on felt eyes and mouth.

SEMINOLE DOLL

TOPSY-EVA,

A black mother of the Old South made a very special doll. It had two heads, but shared a single body. One head was white and the other was black. They were very good friends just like the story book little girls, Topsy and Eva.

tracing paper
pencil
scissors
colored felt
crayon or colored
 felt-tipped marker

liquid white glue in
 an applicator-tip bottle
cotton
scrap fabric
cord

1. With a pencil, trace the doll, Pattern A, the blouse, Pattern B (dotted line), and the face, Pattern C from the book onto tracing paper.
2. Cut out each traced pattern with a scissors.
3. Using the cutouts, trace two doll shapes on brown felt and two on pink felt.
4. Trace four blouse shapes, two of one color, two of another.
5. Trace a face for each doll. Cut out the face pattern from felt which is lighter in color than the doll shapes.
6. Glue a face shape to a pink doll shape and one to a brown doll shape, Fig. a.
7. Cut eyes, noses, and mouths out of felt. Glue a set to each face, Fig. a.

8. Glue two blouse shapes of the same color to the two pink doll shapes. Glue the other blouse shapes to the brown doll shapes, Fig. a.
9. Glue the two "face" doll shapes end to end at the bottom edges, Fig. b. Glue the other two together in a similar fashion. Let all dry.
10. Place the glued dolls with the faces facing down on a table.
11. Spread cotton evenly over the glued doll shapes away from the edges, Fig. c.
12. Squeeze glue along all edges, Fig. d.
13. Place the other attached doll shapes over the glued shapes and press down. Be sure all sides and body shape colors line up.
14. Cut a very long piece of fabric as wide as the width of this page.
15. Make a skirt exactly as explained in the Patchwork Skirt Seminole Doll on page 128.
16. When the skirt has dried, turn it inside out and slip it over one doll's head. The cord should be on the back side. Pull tight and tie.
17. Flip the skirt up or down to change the doll.

TWO DOLLS IN ONE

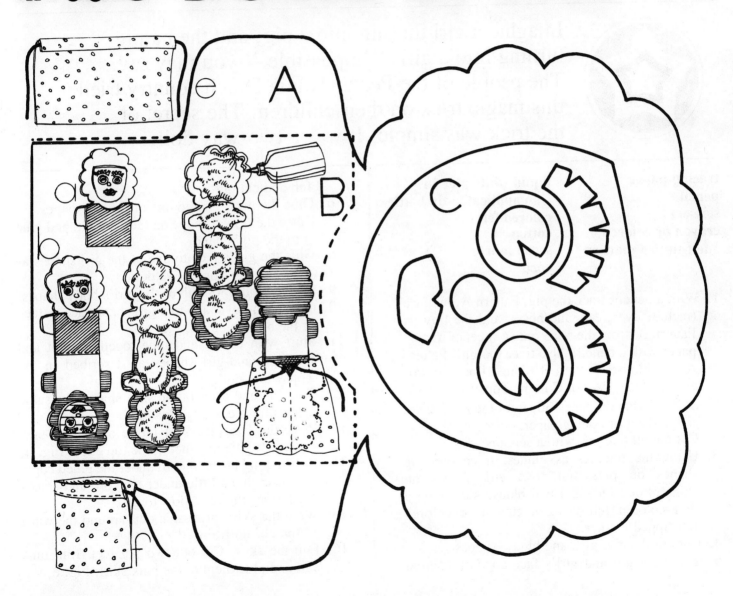

Imagine a girl turning into a pig, and then a pig turning into a girl. "Impossible," you may say. The people of the Pennsylvania Dutch country tried this magic trick on their children. The secret of the trick was simple. It was a two-way doll.

tracing paper
pencil
scissors
crayon or colored
  felt-tipped marker

liquid white glue in
  an applicator-tip bottle
colored felt
cotton
scrap fabric
cord

1. With a pencil, trace the pig, Pattern A, his face (include eyes, ears and nose), and the flower, Pattern B, from the book onto a sheet of tracing paper with a pencil. Also trace the girl, Pattern A, the blouse, Pattern B (dotted line pattern), and the face, Pattern C in the Topsy-Eva, Two Dolls In One on page 130, from the book onto a sheet of tracing paper.
2. Cut out all tracings with a scissors.
3. Using the tracings as guides, trace two pig shapes on pink felt, two girl shapes on skin-colored felt, and two blouse shapes on a dark-colored felt using a crayon or colored felt-tipped marker.
4. Cut out the pig, girl, and blouse shapes.
5. Trace the pig and girl's face on dark-colored

felt and cut out.
6. Glue the pig's face to one of the pig shapes.
7. Trace the flower shape on felt, cut out, and glue it to the pig's hand.
8. Glue the girl's face to one of the girl shapes as shown in the Topsy-Eva doll.
9. Glue a blouse to both of the girl's body shapes.
10. Glue each pig shape to a girl shape face to face at the bottom edges, Fig. a.
11. Stuff with cotton and glue together front and back pig-and-girl shapes as described in the Topsy Eva doll.
12. Cut pink and print fabric skirt shapes the same size as for the Topsy-Eva doll.
13. Place the two pieces of fabric on top of each other and glue together at the top edge, Fig. b.
14. Place a long piece of cord under the glued edge. Squeeze glue a little under the cord and across the fabric, Fig. c. Allow to dry.
15. Wrap the skirt, print-side out, around the waist of the girl doll, Fig. d.
16. Flip the skirt. Cut out two pig feet from pink felt and glue them to the pink skirt, Fig. e.

TWO-WAY DOLL

FLAME DESIGN

The Indians of the Southwest learned how to make different colored dyes a long time ago. They collected berries, blossoms, and other natural things and boiled the color out of them. On crude looms they wove fabric. This fabric was dyed and made into clothing. The flame design stands for the beautiful mountain peaks of the Southwest.

plain colored fabric
cord (or rubber bands)
sand pail
boxed dyes
rubber gloves

1. Fold a piece of fabric back and forth, accordion style, Figs. a and b.
2. Tie the two ends of the folded fabric with cord very tightly, Fig. c. You can use rubber bands.
3. Tie the remaining part of the folded fabric several times, Fig. d. Be sure the cord is tied tightly.
4. Mix a boxed dye according to package directions in a sand pail. If you want a strong color, add little water. If you want a light color add more water.
5. Drop the tied fabric into the sand pail, Fig. e. Leave it in the dye until you have the color you want, Fig. e.
6. Remove the fabric. Protect your hands with rubber gloves.
7. Rinse the fabric under cold water until the water runs clear of dye. Squeeze the fabric continuously.
8. Cut away the cord, and open the fabric.
9. Let the fabric dry completely.
10. If you want extra color, dip each end of the tied fabric into different colored dyes.

TIE-DYED FABRIC

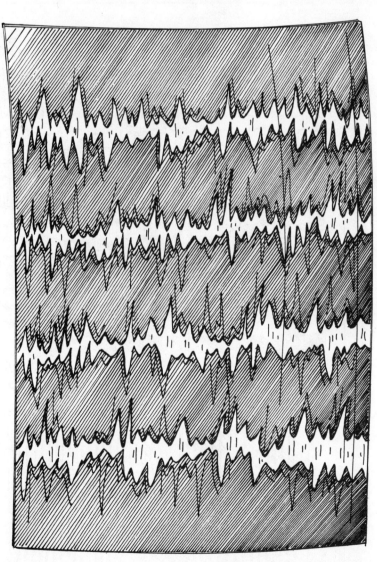

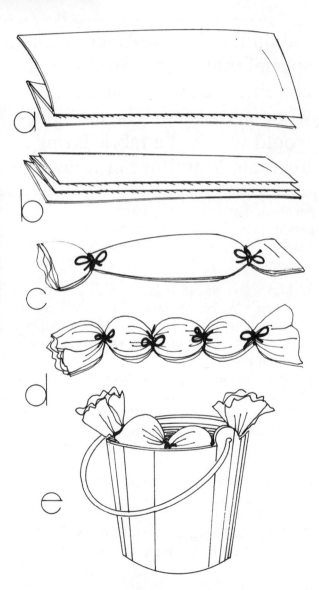

135

RAG WEAVING

Italian families in America had a special craft using worn-out clothing. A loom from scrap wood and string. The children would weave the fabric strips to create beautiful rag weavings.

cardboard
pencil
ruler
scissors

cord
paper
stapler
scrap fabric

1. Make and thread a loom as described in the Chief's Woven Hanging, Fig. a., on page 00.
2. Draw a simple flower on a piece of paper and glue it to a piece of cardboard that is the size of the frame.
3. Staple the drawing to the back of the loom.
4. Cut scrap fabric into thin strips.
5. Weave colored strips into the loom following the lines of the flower, Fig. a. Follow the weaving instructions given in the Chief's Woven Hanging.
6. As you weave keep all ends on the back. When you have finished weaving the flower remove the drawing.
7. Fill in the background with pretty colored fabric strips, Fig. b. Make the weaving tight.

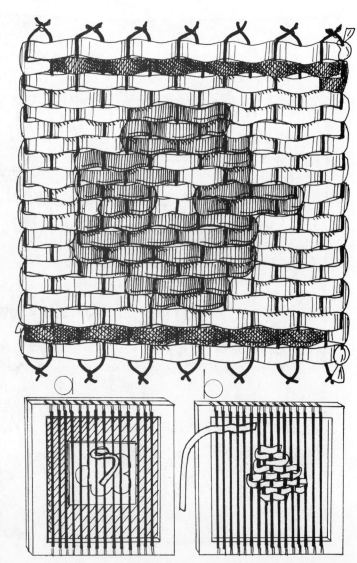

5

NATURE

NATURE

Nature has always been a source for craft ideas and materials. Wrinkly prunes, shiny brown chestnuts, dried corn husks, pine cones, and wild field flowers became decorative and fun-filled objects for American settlers. Many of these "natural" crafts were brought to this country. Others were born on the American soil

KNOTTED CORN

Black plantation workers used their skills to create many things for plantation children. Using dried corn husks and natural hemp, they molded balls of all sizes. Some were used for throwing, others for kick balls. Since natural materials were abundant in the Old South, when an old ball was kicked apart, a new one could be quickly made.

unhusked corn   string
bowl   yarn

1. Remove the husks from fresh corn and stack them in a loose bundle. Tie them together loosely, Fig. a.
2. Dry them in a warm dry place like a closet for about ten days.
3. To start the ball, dip several husks into a bowl of warm water, Fig. b.
4. Wrap one husk into a tight ball, Fig. c.
5. Wrap several more wet husks over the rolled ball, Fig. d.
6. Tie the ball tightly with string and dry it for several days, Fig. e.
7. When the ball is dry, wet more husks, and wrap and tie them around it, Figs. f and g.
8. Dry the ball several days. Continue adding wet husks, tying and drying them until you have the size of ball you want.

9. The last time you tie husks to the ball, do it with colored yarn. Wrap the yarn in all directions.
10. After you have wrapped the ball, start weaving on it by tying an end of a length of colored yarn to the yarn on the ball where two strands cross each other, Fig. h. We will call the bottom part of the crossed strands, Yarn 1.
11. Bring the tied-on yarn over and under Yarn 2, Fig. i.
12. Bring the yarn over to Yarn 3, Fig. j.
13. Bring the yarn under Yarn 3 and over to Yarn 4, Fig. k.
14. Bring the yarn under Yarn 4 and then continue over to Yarn 1. Continue wrapping yarn over and then under the four yarns.
15. Tie the end of the wrapped yarn to a yarn on the ball.
16. Wrap several yarn "crosses" in this fashion, as many as you like.

HUSK THROW=BALL

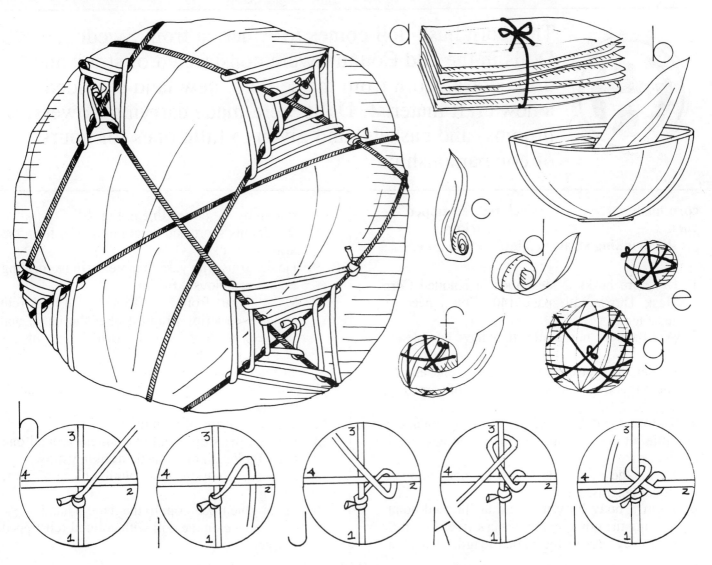

CORN HUSK

This corn husk doll comes to America from Sweden. Dolls in the Old Country were constructed of straw and dried grass. Corn from the settlers' new land provided a new craft material. Dolls were made carrying flowers, brooms, and baskets, and given to little ones for hours of companionship.

corn husk   colored felt-tipped
yarn   markers
plastic drinking straw   liquid white glue

1. Dry corn husks as described in Knotted Corn Husk Throw-Ball, page 140. You'll need at least ten.
2. Wet the corn husks after they have completely dried.
3. Gather the wet corn husks at one end and tie them together with a short length of yarn, Fig. a.
4. To form the doll's head, gather the corn husks a little bit down from the top and tie with yarn, Fig. a.
5. Divide the corn husks below the head into two equal lengths.
6. Form a body by tying yarn at the mid-point, leaving the other length of husk free, Fig. b.
7. Cut away part of the untied length of husk as shown by the dotted line in Fig. b.
8. Divide this shortened length in half to form the arms, Fig. c.
9. Tie the arms with yarn in three sections forming a gathered blouse, Fig. d.
10. Make a scarf from a moistened corn husk (cut in an even strip) wrapped over the head, and crossed in front, Fig. e. Bring ends of the scarf behind the doll's back and cross them just below the waist, Fig. f.
11. Glue the ends of the scarf to each other and to the body.
12. Cut small strips of corn husk.
13. Moisten the strips, and place them around one end of a length of a plastic drinking straw.
14. Tie the husks to the straw with a piece of yarn, Fig. g.
15. Tie or glue the broom to the maid's hand.
16. Draw a face on the doll with colored felt-tipped markers.

SWEEPER MAID

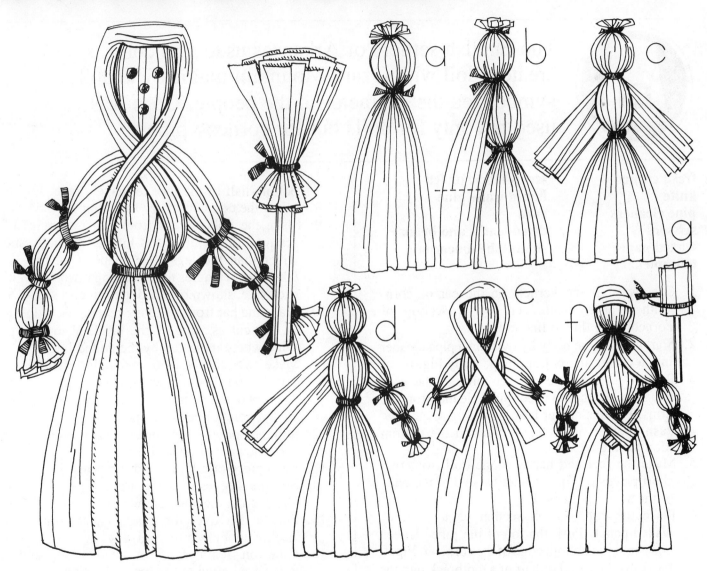

143

CORNCOB HILLYBILLY

The English settlers of Arkansas used corncobs to create a doll with Ozark Mountain magic. The doll symbolized the character of the people. Corn was used not only for dolls but for corncob pipes.

fresh corncob
knife
pipe cleaners
scissors
waxed paper
toothpick

scrap fabric or felt
liquid white glue
cord
dried lentils and beans
small tube macaroni

**1. Cut away all the kernels on the ear of corn With a sharp knife, cut off a section of corncob, see dotted line in Fig. a.

2. Start making the body by twisting a pipe cleaner into a center and bottom loop, study Fig. b.

3. Push a second pipe cleaner through the center loop of the twisted pipe cleaner for the arms. Pull the center loop tight, Fig. c.

4. Push another pipe cleaner through the bottom loop for the legs, Fig. d.

5. Make the feet and hands of the doll from two short pieces of pipe cleaner twisted to the ends of the arms and legs, Fig. e.

6. Place the cut corncob section on a sheet of waxed paper. Push the top of the pipe cleaner body into the bottom edge of the corncob, Fig. f.

7. Press the wide end of half of a toothpick into the bottom half of the face to make a pipe, Fig. f.

8. Allow the corncob to dry for about ten days.

9. Make the doll's dress from two rectangles of scrap fabric or felt cut as long as the body and wider than the legs. See shape X in Fig. g. Glue the rectangles together along two-thirds of each side, shown by the dotted line in shape X.

10. Make the hat from two long rectangles of fabric or felt cut as wide as the head, Y in Fig. g. Glue where indicated by the dotted lines.

11. Make two sleeves from rectangles of fabric or felt as long as the arms, Z in Fig. g. Glue each two together along the sides as shown by the dotted lines in shape Z.

12. Slip the body into the dress, Fig. h. Glue at the top, shown by dotted lines.

13. Tie a piece of cord around the waist.

14. Slip the sleeves over the arms, Fig. i. Glue on the dress in the place shown by the dotted lines.

15. Put the hat over the head. Tie it around the neck with a piece of cord, Fig. j.

16. Glue on lentil eyes, a bead nose, and a marcaroni bowl to the toothpike pipe.

YOKEL GRANNY

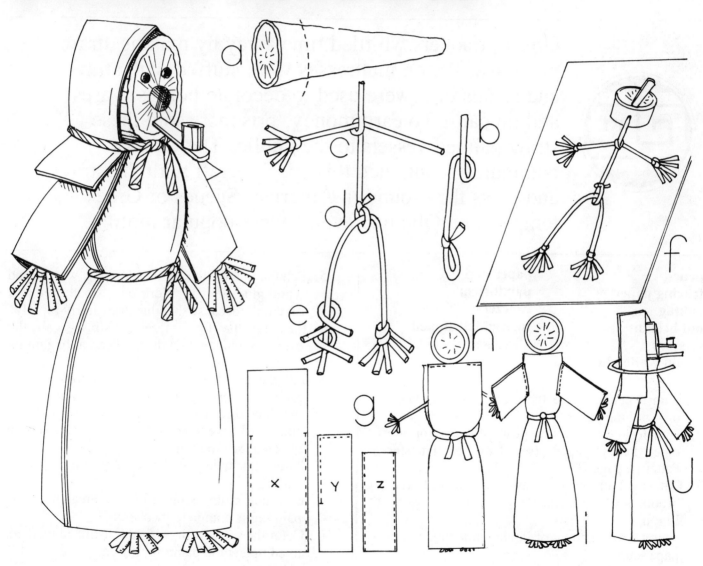

a

b

c

d

e

f

g

x

y

z

h

i

j

145

COLORED-STRAW

Greek prisoners whittled time away by making straw paintings. Prison mattresses were stuffed with straw, and scraps of it were used to decorate bottles, vases, and tin cans. To earn money, prisoners sold these straw-painted vessels to the public. The Greek community continued this special craft with the straw and grass they found in America. Scenes of Greek temples and Olympic events were popular motifs.

pencil
tracing paper
oaktag
old broom
scissors
liquid white glue

paper cup
paintbrush
tweezers
colored felt-tipped
 markers

1. With a pencil, trace the scene from the book onto tracing paper.
2. Transfer the design to a piece of oaktag or any other heavy paper, (see How to Transfer Patterns, page 20).
**3. Cut small pieces of straw from an old wisk broom or a long-handled broom with a scissors, Fig. a.
4. Pour a small amount of liquid white glue into a paper cup.
5. Paint a small area of the drawing with liquid white glue, Fig. b. Work on a small area at a time only because the glue dries fairly rapidly.
6. Pick up the first piece of straw with the tweezers and lay it on the glued area, beginning at one end.
7. Fill the glued area with the remaining straw, each piece placed side by side, all lined up in the same direction, Fig. c. Individual pieces of straw will have to be cut to size in order to fit in the area, see drawing.
8. After this area has been filled in, move to another.
9. Continue gluing straw to scene areas until the painting is completely covered.
10. Color the straw with colored felt-tipped markers to complete the painting, Fig. d.

CLASSICAL SCENE

WRINKLE-FACE

Johnny Appleseed planted his favorite fruit all over the Appalachian Mountains. Even before Johnny's long trek, the Indians enjoyed apples. They used them to create applehead dolls with shriveled faces. So can you.

apple
small knife
potato peeler
salt
cotton
pencils
beads or lentils
paper plate

lemon juice
scissors
cardboard
yarn
toothpicks
plastic bottle
scrap fabric or felt
liquid white glue

**1. Peel the apple, Fig. a.
**2. Cut away the bottom sides of the apple to form a chin, Fig. b.
**3. Scoop out eyes with a potato peeler. Cut out a mouth and nose, Fig. c.
**4. Scoop out the core of the apple from the top. Sprinkle salt inside the hole, then stuff it with cotton, Fig. d.
5. Push a sharpened pencil into the bottom of the apple, Fig. e.
6. Place beads or lentils into the eyes, Fig. e.
7. Place the head on a paper plate. Sprinkle the apple with lemon juice and salt.
8. Let the applehead dry in a dry, warm place for at least two weeks. Some apples do not dry very well so you might make several heads.
9. Cut a small rectangular piece of cardboard, and wrap yarn around it about 20 times.
10. Tie yarn together at the top edge of the cardboard. Cut the yarn at the bottom edge, Fig. f.
11. Remove the yarn from the cardboard and tie it into two pony tails, Fig. g.
12. Attach the hair to the dried applehead with toothpicks, Fig. h.
13. Place the pencil which is stuck in the head into the mouth of a bottle, Fig. i.
14. Wrap scrap fabric or felt around the bottle and tie it around the bottleneck, Fig. j.
15. Cut two hand shapes out of scrap fabric or felt and glue them to two rectangle arms cut from cardboard. Glue the arms to the side of the bottle body, Fig. k.
16. Cut slits into the bottom of the dress. Add a fabric collar, with slits cut into the bottom edge, to the neck, Fig. k.
17. Glue beads around the top and bottom of the dress.

APPLEHEAD DOLL

a

b

c

d

e

f

g

h

i

k

WALNUT=HEAD

Do you shrivel up when someone offers you a prune? Besides eating them, German settlers created craft characters from them based upon figures in the folklore of New York State. A prune doll was supposed to be a sign of good luck. These delicious dolls sported the color and history of German settlements of the New Country.

medium-gauge wire
scissors
box of prunes
2 walnuts
paper
tape

felt or scrap fabric
liquid white glue
ribbon or cord
colored felt-tipped
  marker

***1. Cut a length of the medium-gauge wire about twice as long as your hand, one for each doll.
2. Wrap one end of each wire around the center seam of a walnut and twist wire to wire to hold the nut, Fig. a.
3. Thread two prunes onto each wire around the inside pits to form the body, Fig. b.
4. Twist the remaining wire into a loop. Fig. b.
5. Make a cone hat by rolling a paper semi-circle into a cone, Fig. c. Tape and trim.
6. Make a head scarf by cutting a triangle from scrap fabric, Fig. d.
7. Cut lengths of wire for the arms. Make a loop at one end of each. Thread on two prunes. Fig. e.
8. Wire each arm to the bodies between the walnut

head and the first body prune, Fig. e.
9. Cut longer lengths of wire for the legs.
10. Loop the end of each leg wire, and thread on four prunes.
11. Run the end of wire for each leg through the bottom loop of the body wire and twist in place, Fig. f.
12. For the jacket, cut a piece of scrap fabric the length of the body and wide enough to overlap the arms slightly, Fig. g.
13. Cut a circle out of the center of the jacket rectangle with a short slit, Fig. g.
14. Fold the jacket fabric in half, Fig. h.
15. Make the dress as you just did the jacket, but make the fabric rectangle longer.
16. Slip the jacket and dress onto the dolls.
17. Glue the cone hat to the head of the man and tie a ribbon bow around his neck.
18. Tie the triangle scarf around the head of the lady and add a length of ribbon or cord around her waist.
19. Using a felt-tipped marker, add a face to each.

PRUNE PEASANTS

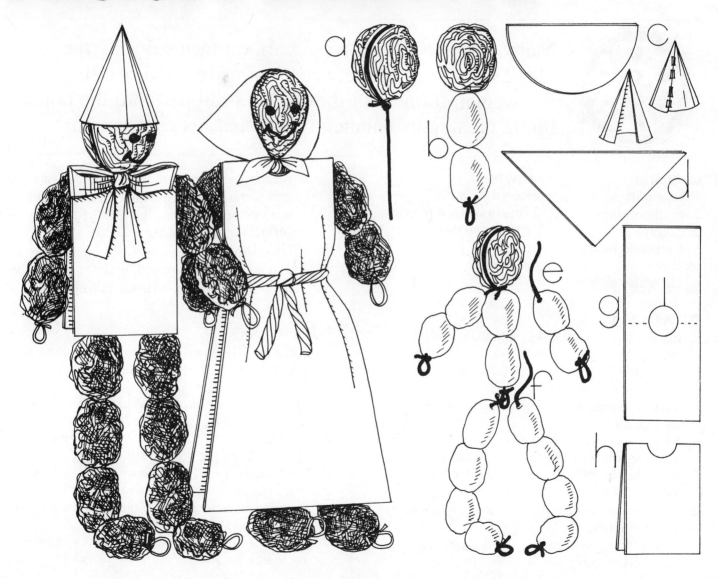

BALANCING POTATO

Many wonderful toys were born on farms during the bleak winter season between harvesting and planting. Norwegian farmers in the Midwest dipped into the potato bin to create this balancing man and his companion.

toothpicks
1 large potato
2 small potatoes
play clay
3 sharpened pencils
feathers
liquid white glue

scissors
colored paper
2 medium-sized potatoes
drinking straws
knife
paper plate

POTATO MAN

1. Insert a toothpick halfway into the top of a large potato.
2. Push the remaining half of the toothpick into a small potato for a head, Fig. a.
3. Roll two small balls of play clay about as large as a quarter.
4. Push the eraser ends of two sharpened pencils into the two balls of clay, one in each.
5. Push the sharpened ends of the pencils into the bottom of the large potato to form legs, Fig. b.
6. Roll two smaller balls of play clay about as large as a dime.
7. Insert the pointed ends of two toothpicks into the balls of clay.

8. Push the blunt ends of the toothpicks into the upper part of the large potato for arms, Fig. c.
9. Insert two feathers into the head, Fig. d. Also insert feathers around the body for a skirt.
10. Glue on colored paper eyes and mouth, Fig. e.
11. Insert a sharpened pencil into the potato between the legs so he will balance upright.

POTATO DOG

1. Put a small potato head to a medium-sized potato body in the same fashion as you did in the Potato Man.
2. Cut a plastic drinking straw into two sections about as long as your index finger.
3. Push the ends of the two sections of straw into the bottom of the potato, see drawing.
**4. Cut a medium-sized potato in half for a base.
5. Place the potato half on a small paper plate.
6. Push the extending ends of plastic straw into the rounded part of the potato base.
7. Add a paper eye, a feather tail, and an end of a toothpick for a snout to the dog's head.

MAN AND HIS DOG

153

THUNDERBIRD IN

The thunderbird was an American Indian evil spirit. It was believed that his mouth spat lightning bolts and when his gigantic wings flapped, thunder was created. The thunderbird was one of the most important symbols to the Indians.

tracing paper
pencil
carbon paper
sheet of sandpaper
fabric dyes
glass jars

spoon
sand
paper towels
liquid white glue
paper cup
paintbrush

1. Trace the thunderbird from the book onto a sheet of tracing paper.
2. Place a sheet of carbon paper over a sheet of fine sandpaper with the carbon side facing down.
3. Place the tracing over the carbon paper.
4. Draw along all lines of the tracing pressing hard on your pencil, Fig. a.
5. Lift off the tracing and the carbon paper. An outline of the thunderbird will remain on the sandpaper.
6. Mix different colors of fabric dyes in glass jars. The less water you use, the stronger the color will be.

7. Spoon sand into each of the jars, Fig. b., and let it remain there for about an hour.
8. Carefully pour out all of the liquid from the jars.
9. Pour the sand onto paper towels and allow it to dry, Fig. c. Keep colors separate.
10. Pour a little liquid white glue into a paper cup.
11. Paint an area of the thunderbird design with the glue, Fig. d.
12. Spoon some dyed sand onto the glued area.
13. When the glue has dried slightly, tilt the picture onto a sheet of paper toweling to remove all excess sand.
14. Move on to another area. Paint this area with glue and spoon another color sand of it. You will probably want to do more than one area in a single color.
15. Continue gluing areas, pouring sand onto them and removing excess sand until the picture is completed.

"DESERT" SANDS

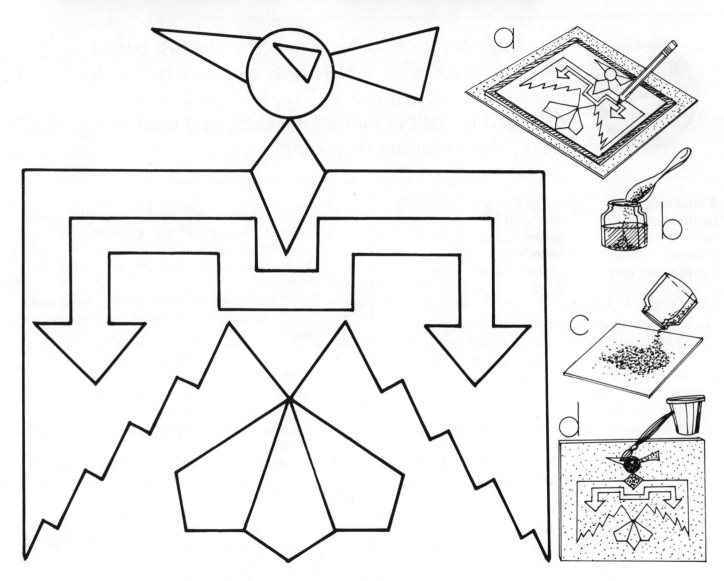

a

b

c

d

SAILOR'S VALENTINE

The English pirates used Key West, the last island in the Florida Keys, as a hideaway and merchant ships landed there occasionally. Tropical shells were collected by sailors journeying there and used in craft projects during their long voyages.

2 matching shells   **scrap fabric**
photographs   **box with lid**
pencil   **poster paints**
scissors   **paintbrush**
liquid white glue   **assorted small shells**

SAILOR'S VALENTINE

1. Place each matching shell over a photograph.
2. Trace around the outer edge of the shells over the area of the photographs you want to display, Fig. a. If your shells have a neck, as does the one in the illustration, trace up to the neck (see X-points).
3. Carefully cut along the drawn out lines on the photographs.
4. Place the matching shells together and glue a small hinge of fabric across the backs of each, Fig. b.
5. When the glue has dried, open the shells.
6. Squeeze glue around the inner edge of each shell, shown by an arrow in Fig. c.
7. Place your photographs over the glued edge of each shell.
8. When the glue has dried, stand the Sailor's Valentine on its side to display the photographs.

SHELL BOX

1. Paint the outside of a box and its lid.
2. Glue tiny shells to the top and sides of the lid.
3. When the glue has dried, place the lid on top of the box.
4. Glue shells on all four sides of the box slightly below the lid.

AND SHELL BOX

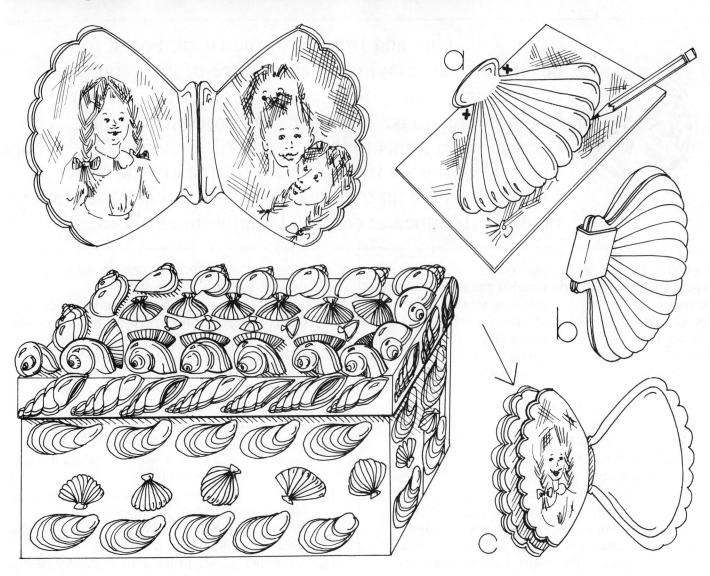

WILD TURKEY WITH

Among the pine and fir trees of the Black Forest live beautiful birds. Having an abundance of pine cones, the German country folk turned these seed hotels into beautiful creations. This craft was brought with the German immigrants to the Catskill Mountains of New York State. The favorite bird to be constructed in the New Country was the turkey, since it was a native American favorite. Its appearance meant happy times ahead.

pencil
corrugated cardboard
scissors
paintbrush
poster paints
paper
liquid white glue

pine cone
wooden game playing-piece
drinking straw
plaster of paris
paper cup
spoon
large bottle cap

1. Draw a circle on corrugated cardboard as large as the tail shown in the book.
**2. Cut out the circle with a scissors, Fig. a.
3. Paint the circle orange, Fig. b.
4. Paint the design, as shown with red, white, and yellow paints, Fig. c. Dry.
5. Place the circle on a sheet of paper positioning it so that when you look through the edge of the corrugated cardboard, you can see completely through the ripply interior. Mark this see-through point as the bottom of the tail.

6. Glue the base of the pine cone to the bottom of the tail, Fig. d.
7. Glue a wooden game playing-piece or any other interesting shape item to the top of the pine cone for a head, Fig. e.
8. Allow the pine cone to dry on the tail overnight.
9. Cut a drinking straw in two with a scissors.
10. Insert the straw sections into the bottom edge of the tail below the pine cone body, Fig. f. Be sure that they are fairly close together.
11. Mix a small amount of plaster of paris in a paper cup with enough water to make a mixture with the consistency of heavy cream.
12. Spoon a little plaster into a large bottle cap, almost up to the top, Fig. g.
13. When the plaster has begun to set, push the straw legs into it, Fig. h.
14. Allow the plaster to harden completely before displaying your turkey.

A COLORFUL TAIL

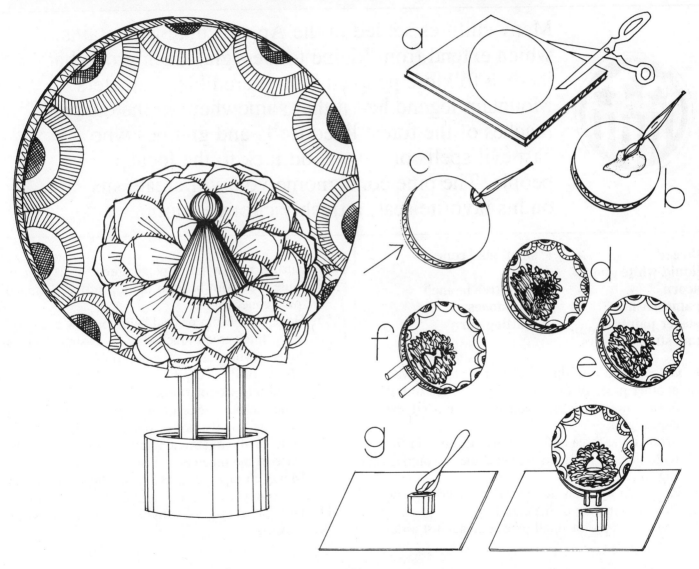

APPALACHIAN FOREST

Many cultures settled in the Appalachian Mountains, which extend from Maine to Georgia. Each group had its own folklore peopled with incredible characters. Mountain legend had it that somewhere in the darkest reaches of the forest lived trolls and gnomes who cast evil spells or gave good luck to the local people. The pine cone gnome you will create sits on his favorite seat, a freshly cut tree stump.

thread
liquid white glue
acorn
paintbrush
poster paints
tiny straw flowers

small pine cone
saw
thick tree branch
tiny stones
knitting yarn

1. Gather lengths of thread at their center, tie with another piece of thread, and glue to the top of an acorn from which you have removed the cap, Fig. a.
2. Arrange the thread into a pretty hairdo over the wide sides of the acorn and glue the cap onto it, Fig. b.
3. Paint two eyes on the acorn and glue a straw flower to the top of the cap, Fig. c.
4. Press the top of a small pine cone against a flat surface so that the top petals spread apart, Fig. d.
5. Glue the acorn head to the top of the flattened pine cone, Fig. e.
**6. Have your Mom or Dad help you saw a section off a thick tree branch, Fig. f. It should be as long as your hand. A small tin can filled with plaster of Paris can be a substitute.
7. Stand this section upright.
8. Glue the pine cone to the top of the section as indicated by the dotted line in Fig. g.
9. Glue small stones and straw flowers around the base of the pine cone, Fig. g.
10. Make clumps of grass from small pieces of knitting yarn. Unravel and fluff up the ends.
11. Glue the clumps of yarn between the stones and flowers.

PINE CONE GNOME

161

GAELIC PRESSED-

The sweet smell of a field of purple heather made the hard chores on an Irish farm easier. The same hard labor accompanied the Irish settlers to America. Pressing heather between the pages of favorite books preserved a bit of Ireland. Pressed flower arrangements were hung on every wall.

tiny field flowers, grass, clover
waxed paper
heavy books
scissors
cardboard
pencil
small paintbrush
poster paints
paper
tweezers
liquid white glue
paper cup
clear plastic wrap
tape

1. Pick flat flowers, grass, and clover.
2. Place the flowers between two sheets of waxed paper and then inside a book, Fig. a.
3. Place more books on top of the first book and press the flowers for ten days, Fig. b.
4. Cut a rectangle out of cardboard.
5. Draw a line down and across the center of the cardboard, Fig. c.
6. Draw an oval by connecting the arms of the cross—the X-points, Fig. d.—with a curved line.
7. Draw a second oval inside the first equally spaced on all sides, Fig. d.
**8. Cut out the outer and inner ovals.
9. Paint the frame a light color. Paint tiny flowers at three points, Fig. e.
10. Cut a paper oval larger than the oval opening on the frame, Fig. f.
11. Remove the flowers from the book. Turn upside down with a tweezers, Fig. g.
12. Pour liquid white glue into a paper cup. Carefully brush glue with a small paintbrush to the backs of the flowers and clover, Fig. h.
13. Lift the glued flowers with a tweezers. Place them glue side down on the paper oval in a pretty design, Fig. i.
14. Place the floral design between two pieces of waxed paper and dry them flat in a book.
15. Cut a piece of clear plastic wrap larger than the opening on the frame and tape to the back of the frame, Fig. j.
16. Glue or tape the dried flowers on the paper to the back of the frame, Fig. k.

FLOWER NOSEGAY

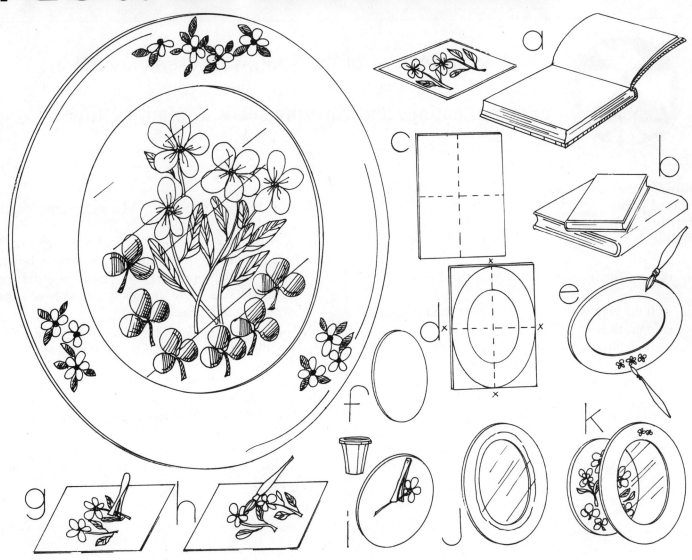

ROLLED CLAY COIL

The Pueblo Indians of the Southwest used clay more than twelve hundred years ago. They made clay pots for cooking, eating, and carrying seeds at planting time.

air-dry modeling clay
waxed paper
bowl
butter

1. Place a small piece of clay on a sheet of waxed paper.
2. Roll the clay with the palm of your hand to form a long, thin rope, Fig. a.
3. Turn a bowl upside down. Spread the outside of the bowl with softened butter, Fig. b.
4. Place one end of the clay rope at the center of the top of the upside down bowl. Wind the rope around itself and the bowl, Fig. c. The clay should be kept very wet by dipping your fingers in water as you work with it. Press the rope firmly against itself as you wrap it around the bowl.

5. Roll another rope of clay about the same length and thickness as the first.
6. Wet the new clay rope and press one end of it against the end of the previous one on the bowl.
7. Wrap this new rope of clay just as you did the first. Be sure there are no spaces between the wrapped coils, Fig. d.
8. Continue making clay ropes and winding them around the bowl until it is completely covered, Fig. e.
9. Allow the clay to dry until it is very hard.
10. Turn the bowl rightside up, Fig. f.
11. Carefully lift the bowl from the dried, coiled clay, Fig. g.
12. The coil bowl can be left as it is or you can paint it in natural colors. Use it as a catch-all, or a planter for your Mom.

CEREMONIAL BOWL

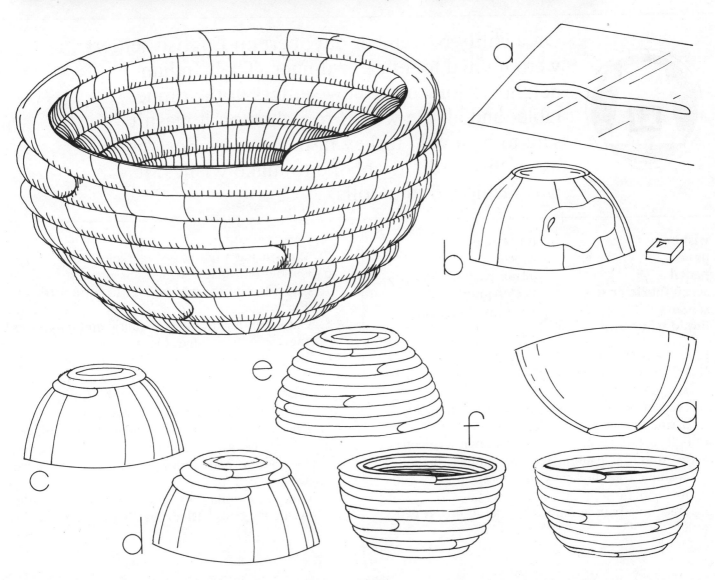

a

b

c

d

e

f

g

LUCKY WISHBONE

On a chilly November day, certain English settlers were invited to a turkey dinner. Their Indian neighbors joined the new settlers at the dinner table, and all ate well. From then on it wasn't safe to be a wild turkey in the woods. Besides using this bird's wishbone to make wishes, it was fashioned into dolls.

wishbone
paper
pencil
scrap fabric or felt
scissors
liquid white glue

tiny beads
acorn
paintbrush
poster paints
felt-tipped marker

1. Dry a wishbone.
2. When completely dry, place the wishbone on a sheet of paper.
3. Trace around the wishbone with a pencil, Fig. a, and put the bone aside.
4. Follow the basic shape of the drawn wishbone to draw a pattern for the Indian brave's costume (see the heavy line in Fig. b). Cut out this pattern.
5. Trace this pattern onto scrap fabric or felt two times using a felt-tipped marker.
6. Cut out two shapes with a scissors.
7. Cut slits into the bottom legs to form a fringe, Fig. c.
8. Cut a thin length of scrap fabric and make slits into the bottom edge, Fig. c.
9. Glue the length to the center of one of the costume halves and trim even with the sides. Also glue tiny beads to the top half, Fig. d.
10. Place the wishbone on a sheet of paper.
11. Glue an acorn to the top of the wishbone, Fig. e.
12. When the glue has dried, paint a face on the acorn and shoes on the legs of the wishbone, Fig. f.
13. Glue the Indian brave's costume, with the wishbone body inside, together, Fig. g.

INDIAN BRAVE

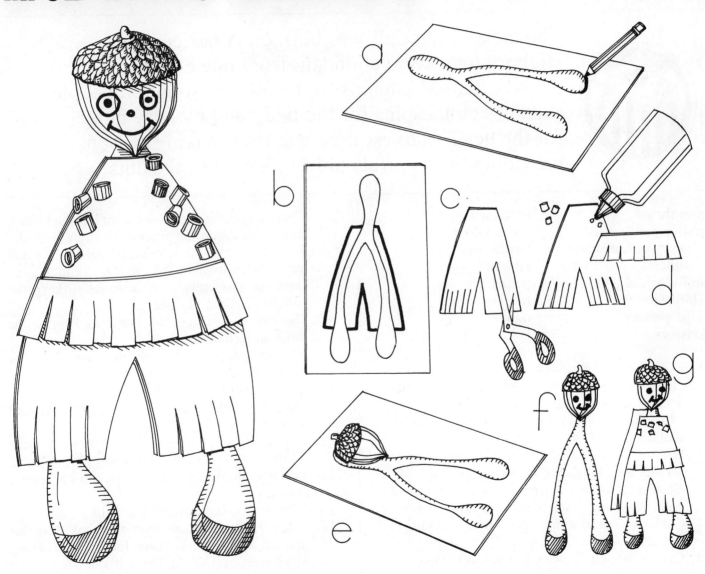

HICKORY NUT

The hickory nut doll was born on American soil. Hickory trees were abundant from one end of the Appalachian Mountains to the other. Mountain people used old clothespins for the body and hickory nuts for the head. Harvest time was doll-making season, providing the squirrels didn't hide all of the nuts.

paintbrush
poster paint
hickory nut, acorn or
   filbert
liquid white glue
clothespin
pipe cleaner
scissors

scrap felt
scrap fabric
needle and thread
ribbon
pencil
tracing paper
paper

1. Paint eyes and a mouth on either a hickory nut, filbert, or acorn. The pointed end of the nut will be the nose, Fig. a.
2. Glue the nut head to the top of a wooden clothespin, Fig. b.
3. When the glue has dried, wrap a pipe cleaner around the clothespin where it joins the head. Start at the front and wrap the two ends around each other at the back to form the arms, Fig. c.
4. Cut hands out of scrap fabric or felt and glue to the ends of the arms, Fig. c.
5. Cut a fabric circle twice as large as the nut.

**6. Thread a needle and knot the end of the thread.
7. Sew a running stitch around the circle, Fig. d.
8. Place the fabric circle over the head of the doll and pull the thread tightly to form a cap, Fig. e.
9. Sew the last stitch several times to keep the stitches and hat in place.
10. Cut two pieces of scrap fabric as long as the body to form a dress.
11. Thread a needle and sew the two pieces of fabric together with a running stitch, Fig. f.
12. Turn the skirt inside out.
**13. Thread a needle and sew a running stitch around one opening, Fig. g.
14. Slip the dress over the body and up to the head of the doll. Pull the thread tightly, Fig. h.
15. Sew the dress shut at the neck with several stitches.
16. Tie a ribbon bow around the waist.
17. Trace the basket shape from the book. Use this tracing to cut a basket from felt or paper. Hang the basket over one of the doll's hands.

CLOTHESPIN DOLL

a

b

c

d

e

f

g

CHESTNUT BOY

Czechoslovakian immigrants were surprised to see chestnuts growing in America. In the Northeast, Czechs not only roasted them, but turned them into dolls.

pencil	paper cup
chestnut	spoon
scissors	bottle cap
drinking straws	paintbrush
liquid white glue	poster paints
plaster of paris	toothpicks

1. Poke two holes on the bottom end of a chestnut with a sharp pencil, Fig. a.
2. Cut two small lengths from a drinking straw and push them into the holes, Fig. b. Add a dab of glue to each hole to keep the straws in place.
3. Mix plaster of paris with water in a paper cup until the mixture looks like heavy cream.
4. Spoon a little plaster of paris into a bottle cap, almost to the top, Fig. c.
5. When the plaster begins to harden, push the straw legs into it, Fig. d.
6. When the plaster is hard, paint a white face onto the nut with silly eyes, nose and mouth.
7. Insert toothpicks into the head, one on each side, with the blunt end sticking out.

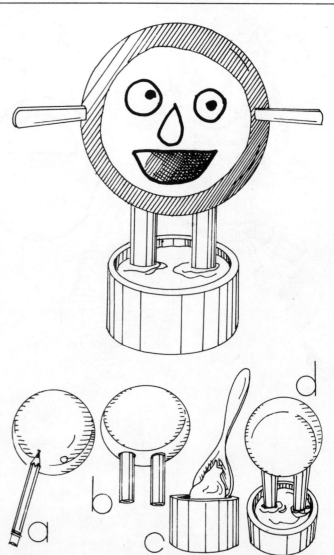

170

6

PAINT

PAINT

People have been painting ever since there have been people—remember primitive man's decorated caves? Paint was made originally from natural things. Berries, flowers, and sand were boiled or ground to produce a strong dye. Today all you have to do is go to the store and buy as many jars of paint as you need. Many painted treasures and paint crafts were brought to America. If you like to paint, you'll love this chapter.

REPEATED EMBLEM

The Japanese handprinted exquisite designs on fabric.
They brought this skill with them to America.
Textile printing at home is relatively simple.
You will enjoy making this lovely hanging banner
worthy of an emperor's palace.

tracing paper
pencil
heavy cardboard
scissors

liquid white glue
white fabric
poster paints
paintbrush

1. With a pencil, trace the design Patterns A, B, and C, minus the circles from the body onto tracing paper. Transfer the patterns to cardboard (see information on How to Transfer a Pattern, page 20).
2. Trace and transfer to cardboard six circles from the book just as you did above.
**3. Cut out the designs and circles with a scissors, Fig. a.
4. Glue the three cutout designs onto three of the cardboard circles, Fig. b.
5. Lay a piece of white fabric flat on a table or on the floor.
6. Brush a coating of poster paint on a circle that doesn't have a design on it.

7. Using the cardboard circle as a printer, press the painted side of the circle onto one corner of the fabric, Fig. c. Press hard.
8. Carefully lift the circle off the fabric.
9. Brush a coating of poster paint on the raised pattern of one design-circle. Be careful not to get any paint on the circle.
10. Press the painted design over the printed circle on the fabric, Fig. d.
11. Carefully lift the circle off the fabric.
12. Print a row of circles and designs across the top of the fabric.
13. Cut a long, skinny rectangle from cardboard.
14. Paint one side of the cardboard with poster paint and use it to print a line under the circles.
15. Continue printing rows of circles and designs with lines underneath them. You can use all of one design in a row or mix the designs.
16. Finish off the printed fabric by turning under a little of each edge and gluing it to the back of the fabric for a hem.

TEXTILE PRINTING

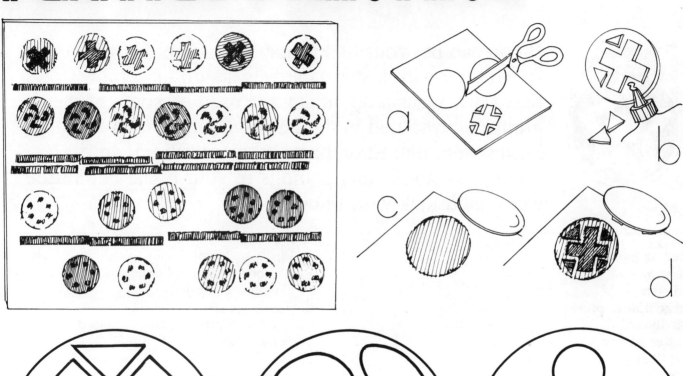

LUCKY STAR

"You can bet your lucky star," is a popular saying. A hex sign with a star pattern is a sign of good luck. Hex signs were made and used by some of the groups who settled in the Pennsylvania Dutch country. Hexes were placed on barns to ward off evil spirits. There may not be any demons in your home but a little extra good luck won't hurt.

tracing paper
pencil
scissors
large dinner plate
cardboard
poster paints
paintbrush
stick-on picture hanger

1. With a pencil, trace the large and small star patterns from the book onto a sheet of tracing paper.
2. Transfer the stars onto a sheet of cardboard (see How to Transfer a Pattern, page 20).
3. Cut out the cardboard stars with a scissors.

4. Place a large dinner plate on a sheet of cardboard and trace around it.
5. Cut out the circle.
6. Place the large star on the center of the cardboard circle. Trace around it, Fig. a, and set it aside.
7. Place the small star in the area between two points of the larger star and trace around it, Fig. b.
8. Using the small star as a guide, draw a star between every two points of the large star, Fig. c.
9. Paint the background of the hex sign a bright color and the stars white or yellow.
10. Paint a zigzag design around the outer edge of the circle, Fig. c.
11. Add a stick-on picture hanger to the back of the hex sign for hanging.

HEX BARN SIGN

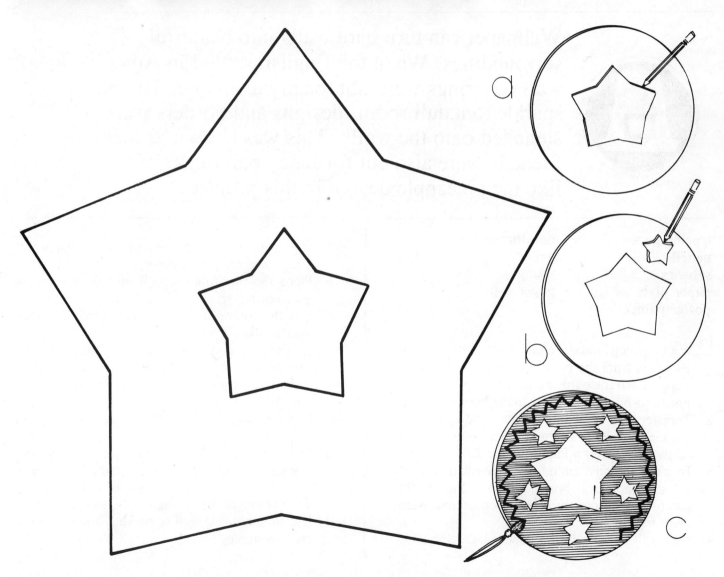

THEORUM PINEAPPLE

Wallpaper can turn bare walls into beautiful surroundings. When the English settled in America, wall coverings were not locally available. To add sparkle to a dull room, designs and borders were stenciled onto the walls. This was known as theorum. Stencils were also cut for fancy paintings, just like the pineapple design in this project.

tracing paper
pencil
scissors
paper plate
poster paints

paintbrush
paper
sponge
paper cup

1. With a pencil, trace the pineapple pattern, in all its parts, from the book onto a sheet of tracing paper. Also trace the border design, the pattern enclosed by the thin lines in the book.
2. Transfer the pineapple onto one piece of drawing paper and the border onto another (How to Transfer a Pattern, page 20).
3. To make stencils, cut out the individual parts of the pineapple and border designs, Fig. a. Be careful not to cut into the paper beyond each area, Fig. a.
4. Pour a little paint into a paper plate. Spread it

thin with a small paintbrush and some water (don't add too much water).
5. Place the pineapple stencil on the center of a piece of paper.
6. Dab the corner of a moist sponge into the paint on the plate.
7. Dab the painted corner of the sponge into one cutout area of the pineapple stencil. Apply paint mostly along the edge of the cutout area, Fig. b.
8. Dip the other corner of the sponge into a paper cup full of water.
9. Dab the center of the painted area with the wet corner and outwards towards the edges. Blend the paint so that the color is lighter in the middle and darker at the edges, Fig. c.
10. Use the border stencil to make a border around the pineapple, Fig. d.

STENCIL PRINTING

TWO BUTTERFLIES

A silk painting begins with the silk worm. The worm spins a cocoon which is collected along with thousands of other cocoons. The cocoons are spun into thread. The thread is then woven into a soft, shiny fabric that is called silk. The Chinese discovered silk a long time ago. They painted pictures on it and decorated their homes with the paintings just as you are going to do.

tracing paper
pencil
carbon paper
shiny fabric
poster paints

paintbrush
liquid white glue
long drinking sraw
piece of fringe
cord

1. Cut a piece of shiny fabric as wide as this page and a little longer.
2. With a pencil, trace the butterfly, branch and flower design from the book onto a sheet of tracing paper.
3. Place the carbon side of a sheet of carbon paper over the fabric.
4. Place the tracing on the center of the carbon paper, with the short sides of the fabric on the top and bottom.

5. Draw over the lines of the tracing with a sharpened pencil, Fig. a.
6. Remove the papers.
7. Paint in the designs on the fabric with pink, green, and blue poster paints. Use different shades of each color.
8. Fold over the bottom and sides of the fabric a little bit, and glue them to the back, Fig. b.
9. Place a drinking straw at the top of the backside of the fabric. Fold the top edge of the fabric over the straw and glue it down, Fig. c.
10. When the glue has dried, turn the fabric over, painted side facing you.
11. Glue a fringe to the bottom edge, Fig. d.
12. Tie a piece of cord to the ends of the straw for hanging, Fig. d.

PAINTED ON SILK

NIGHT IN THE WOODS

Ukrainian people painted beautiful pictures on glass. Pictures were painted backwards on one side of a pane of glass. When you looked at the unpainted side, the picture looked correct. It is like painting your reflection in a mirror or a pond. Glass painting isn't as confusing as it sounds. Your creation will be worthy of being hung in a museum.

cardboard
pencil
ruler
scissors
clear plastic wrap
cellophane tape
tracing paper

black felt-tipped
  marker
poster paints
small paintbrush
scouring cleanser
paper

1. Cut a cardboard rectangle a little larger than this page.
2. Use a ruler to draw a small rectangle within the larger. It shouldn't be too much smaller than the original rectangle.
**3. Cut out the inner rectangle to form a frame, Fig. a.
4. Cut a piece of clear plastic wrap larger than the opening of the frame.
5. Tape the plastic wrap over the opening on all sides. Tape it tightly, Fig. b.
6. With a pencil, trace the drawing from the book on a sheet of tracing paper with a pencil.
7. Lay the tracing face up on a table. Place the plastic wrapped frame over the tracing, taped side facing you.
8. Trace the drawing onto the clear plastic wrap with a black felt-tipped marker. Draw the tree trunks up to the top edge of the frame's opening, Fig. c.
9. Mix a little scouring cleanser with the poster paints and paint in the marker drawing on the plastic wrap with a paintbrush, Fig. d.
10. When paints have dried, cut a piece of paper slightly smaller than the frame and tape it to the back to cover up the tape. Turn your painting over and enjoy.

GLASS PAINTING

BOWL OF FRUIT

The English painted pictures on glass just like the Ukrainians. During the Victorian Era in England, glass paintings were very popular. Religious scenes and still lives shimmered when silver tinsel was added to the back of the paintings.

oaktag or other
  lightweight cardboard
pencil
ruler
scissors
clear plastic wrap
cellophane tape

tracing paper
black poster paint
scouring cleanser
small paintbrush
colored indelible ink
  felt-tipped markers
aluminum foil

1. Cut out a cardboard rectangle a little larger than this page.
2. Use a ruler to draw a smaller rectangle within the larger one. It shouldn't be too much smaller than the original rectangle.
**3. Cut out the inner rectangle to make a frame just as you did for the Night In The Woods Glass Painting on page 182.
4. Cut a piece of clear plastic wrap a little larger than the frame opening. Tape it tightly over the opening.
5. Trace the bowl of fruit drawing from the book onto a sheet of tracing paper.

6. Lay the frame with the tape side facing you over the drawing.
7. Mix a little scouring cleanser with black poster paint, and paint in all of the background on the plastic wrap with a paintbrush, Fig. a.
8. Color in all of the fruit with colored felt-tipped markers, Fig. b. Indelible markers work best. You may have to draw over areas several times if you use watercolor markers.
9. Cut out another piece of cardboard the same size as the frame, for a backing.
10. Cut a piece of aluminum foil the same size as the backing.
11. Crumple up the foil into a loose ball, Fig. c. Uncrumple the foil but don't flatten it too much.
12. Tape the foil to the cardboard with the shiny side facing you.
13. Place the framed design over the foil with the taped side facing down, Fig. d.
14. Use a little tape on all sides to hold the frame and the foiled cardboard together.

TINSEL PAINTING

FOLK ART HEARTS AND

The Pennsylvania Dutch painted traditional designs on furniture, in fact, anything that had a flat surface. Two of the more popular designs were the heart and the tulip. The heart stands for friendship and love, and the tulip is a popular flower.

box with cover
poster paints
paintbrush
tracing paper
pencil
carbon paper

1. Paint a box and its cover with a light colored poster paint, Fig. a.
2. Trace the heart and tulip designs from the book onto a sheet of tracing paper.
3. Place the carbon side of a sheet of carbon paper on the cover of the box. Place the tracing paper on top of the carbon paper, Fig. b.
4. Draw over the lines of the tracing with a sharpened pencil. Press hard.
5. Lift up the carbon paper and the tracing to reveal your traced design, Fig. c.
6. Using poster paints, paint the heart red, the leaves green, the tulips orange and yellow, and the dots white, Fig. d.
7. Transfer the design to the sides of the box just as you did the cover.
8. Paint the designs on the sides just as you did the cover.

FLOWERS BOX

DECORATE UTENSILS

 Rosemailing was a folk art of Norway. It simply means "rose painting." Anything with a flat surface can be used for a rosemailing project. Ask Mom or Dad for a kitchen utensil that isn't needed anymore. Everyone will be surprised to see how beautiful it will look when you finish this craft.

scouring cleanser
poster paints
metal utensil (cup, coffee
 pot, funnel, tray, etc.)
paintbrush
tracing paper
pencil
carbon paper
cellophane tape

1. Add a little scouring cleanser to a light colored poster paint and paint an old metal utensil.

2. With a pencil, trace the design from the book onto a sheet of tracing paper.
3. Tape a piece of carbon paper, carbon side down, to the area of the utensil that will be rosemailed. You may have to trim the paper for a small object like a funnel.
4. Tape the tracing over the carbon paper.
5. Draw along the lines of the drawing with a sharpened pencil. Press hard.
6. Remove the tracing and the carbon paper from the utensil.
7. Paint in the design with bright colors.

WITH ROSEMAILING

HANDPAINTED

China is the name of an Asian country and also a type of ceramic ware. The Chinese have been making fine china for centuries, as well as lacquer ware, which is wood coated with many layers of varnish. They brought these bowls, plates, and vases with them for their American homes.

paper plate
poster paints
paintbrush
tracing paper
pencil

carbon paper
liquid white glue
paper cup
stick-on picture hanger

1. Paint a paper plate with red poster paint.
2. With a pencil, trace the drawing from the book onto a sheet of tracing paper with a pencil.
3. Place the carbon side of a sheet of carbon paper on the center of the plate.
4. Place the tracing over the carbon paper, Fig. a. The drawing should be facing you.
5. Draw along the lines of the tracing with a sharpened pencil.
6. Remove the tracing and the carbon paper.
7. Paint the design with poster paints, Fig. b: the grass and leaves should be green, the tree brown, the flowers pink, and the bird blue and white, Fig. b.
8. Pour liquid white glue into a paper cup.
9. Paint the entire plate with glue, Fig. c. It is best to use a large brush and paint in one direction. If you paint the glue back and forth, the painted design will smudge.
10. Let the glue dry until it is clear.
11. Give the plate a second coating of blue.
12. Add a stick-on picture hanger to the back of the plate for hanging.

LACQUERED PLATE

EBONY FLORAL DISH

A Mexican kitchen is a happy place. The walls are gaily decorated with handcarved wooden dishes painted with garlands of red, yellow, and orange flowers.

tracing paper
pencil
carbon paper
paper plate
poster paints
paintbrush
stick-on picture hanger.

1. With a pencil, trace the flower design from the book onto a sheet of tracing paper.
2. Place the carbon side of a sheet of carbon paper on the inside of a paper plate.
3. Place the carbon paper with the drawing facing you.
4. Draw along all lines of the drawing with a pencil. Press hard.
5. Remove the tracing and the carbon paper.
6. Paint the flowers with red, orange, and pink poster paints. Paint the leaves green.
7. Paint the background with black poster paint.
8. Add a stick-on picture hanger to the back of the plate near the top for hanging.

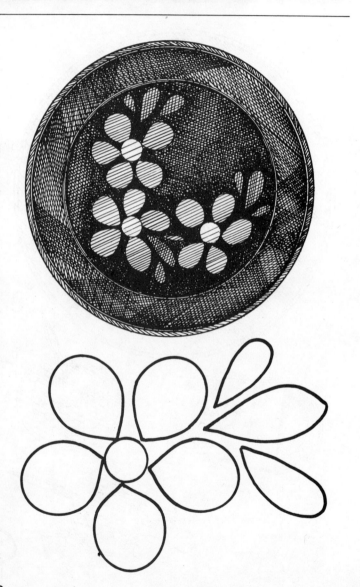

7

PAPER

PAPER

Paper, as we all know, has played a major role in
spreading the printed word, and has helped
the world learn about itself. It has also been
sculptured, cut, and folded into many beautiful
craft objects. Origami dolls, wycinanki paper cuts
and cobweb Valentine cards are just three of the
paper crafts brought to America.

MONI-KIRI

The Japanese showed their family pride by displaying family crests. Each family name had its own design and colors. In times of war, the crest was an easy way to identify a friend or a foe. The Japanese who settled in America kept this tradition alive. Family crests are cut from paper, and this art is known as Mon-Kiri.

tracing paper
pencil
scissors
compass

black paper
liquid white glue or paste
white paper

CIRCLE CREST

1. Trace Pattern A (heavy dotted and solid outline) from the book onto a sheet of tracing paper with a pencil.
2. Cut out the pattern with a scissors.
3. Place the point of a compass on Point X in the drawing which include Pattern A, and the pencil on point Z. Draw a circle using this measurement on a sheet of black paper.
4. Cut out the circle, Fig. a.
5. Fold the circle in half, Fig. b.
6. Fold the half-circle in three equal parts Fig. c (shown by the dotted lines in Fig. b.).
7. Fold the folded circle in half, Fig. d, shown by the dotted lines in Fig c.

8. Place the pattern over the folded circle and trace around it with a pencil, Fig. e.
9. Cut out all areas corresponding to the shaded areas, Fig. e.
10. Open the circle and glue or paste it to a piece of white paper.

OVAL CREST

1. Cut out a piece of black paper to form a rectangle that is twice as long and high as pattern B.
2. Fold this rectangle in half, Fig. f, and then in half again, Fig. g. The paper will look as it does in Fig. h.
3. Trace and cut out Pattern B just as you did Pattern A.
4. Place the pattern on the folded paper as shown in Fig. i, and trace around it.
5. Cut out, and glue down the oval crest just as you did with the circle crest.

FAMILY CRESTS

PINPRICKED

Valentine's Day was the paper craftsman's favorite holiday at the turn of the century. The Pennsylvania Dutch made particularly lovely Valentines with a technique known as pinpricking. The card makers would prick holes through paper to create added detail. The end result was a Valentine card that you would remember in your heart forever.

compass   scissors
lightweight paper   newspaper
tracing paper   safety pin
pencil

1. Place the point of a compass on the X point of the Pattern (heavy solid and dotted outlines) in the book, and the pencil at the Z point.
2. With the compass at this setting, draw a circle on lightweight paper.
3. Cut out the circle, Fig. a, and fold it in half, Fig. b.
4. Fold the half-circle in half, Fig. c, and then in half again, Fig. d.
5. Trace the Pattern from the book onto a sheet of tracing paper with a pencil. Cut it out carefully.
6. Place the cut tracing over the folded circle and trace around the pattern with a pencil, Fig. e.
7. Cut out all the shaded areas corresponding to those in Fig. e.
8. Open the cut paper circle and lay it flat on several sheets of newspaper.
**9. Hold an open safety pin very carefully in your hand and poke tiny holes into the cut paper in the places indicated by the dots in the Pattern, Fig. f.
10. If you hold your pinpricked design in front of a light you will see shimmering dots of light.

DOT VALENTINE

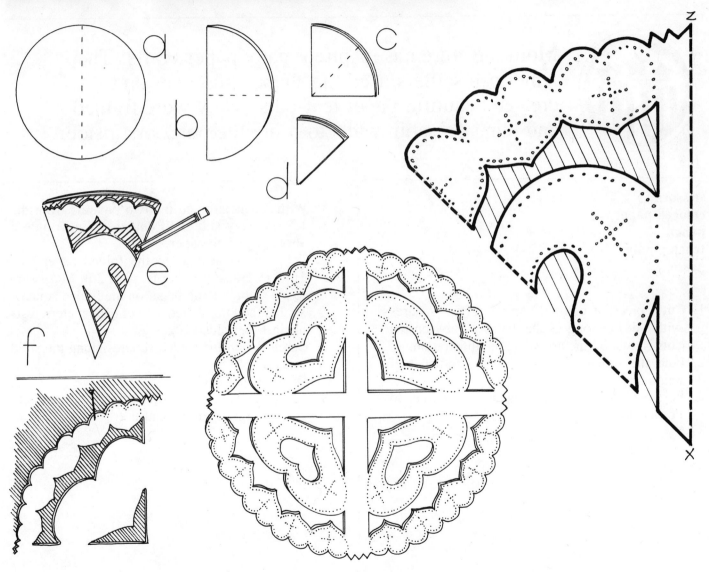

FOUR LEAF-CUTS

 Mother Nature has inspired many paper crafts. The American settlers used the shapes of leaves and created beautiful paper leaf-cuts. They were framed and hung on cabin walls to bring the outdoors inside.

scissors
colored paper
pencil
tracing paper
paste

1. Cut a piece of colored paper into two squares with sides as long as the distance between the dots shown by the arrows in the illustration.
2. Fold the squares in half, Fig. a, and in half again, Fig. b.
3. Fold each square in half again from corner to corner, Fig. c.

4. With a pencil, trace the two patterns from the book (heavy solid and dotted outlines) onto a sheet of tracing paper.
5. Transfer the designs to the folded paper (see How to Transfer Patterns, page 20). Make sure to place the tracing paper on the folded squares so that the long dotted side of each pattern rests against the folded edges.
6. Carefully cut the folded squares along the solid lines, Fig. d.
7. Open the paper to see your leaf-cut.
8. Paste the leaf-cut to a square piece of paper cut a little larger than the leaf-cut.

ALL-IN-A-SQUARE

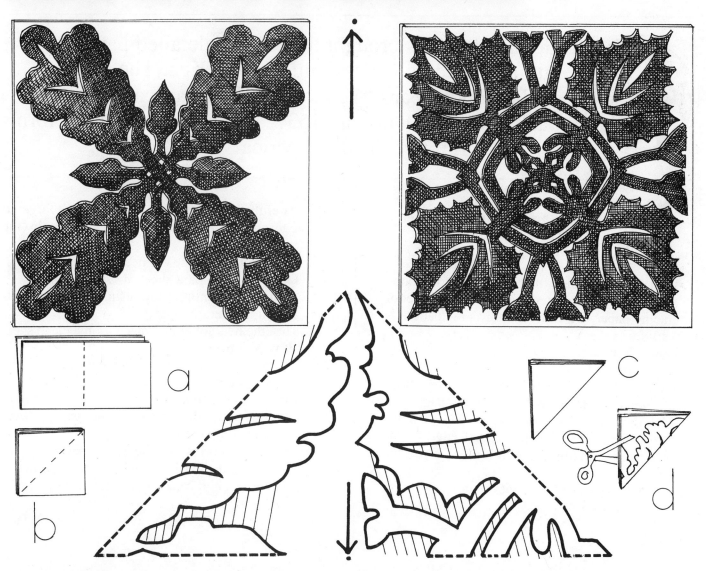

a

b

c

d

SCHERENSCHNITTE

German families brought the craft of detailed paper cutting called Scherenschnitte to America. The word itself simply means "scissor cut." The art can be traced back to Germany around 1631. It is one of the oldest forms of paper craft to come to America.

tracing paper
pencil
white paper
scissors

waxed paper
black felt-tipped marker
rubber cement

1. With a pencil, trace the pattern from the book (heavy solid and dotted outline) onto a sheet of tracing paper. Be extra careful as the pattern is very fancy.
2. Fold a long sheet of white paper in half along the shorter side.
3. Transfer the tracing onto the folded paper, Fig. a. (see How to Transfer Patterns, page 20). Make sure to place the tracing paper on the folded square so that the dotted edge of the pattern rests against the folded edge of the paper.
4. Cut out the heart from the white paper very carefully with a scissors, Fig. b. Don't forget to cut out all the shaded areas shown in the pattern.
5. Slowly open out the cut heart.
6. Place the heart on a sheet of waxed paper.
7. "Paint" the entire heart using the black felt-tipped marker.
8. Turn the heart over and place it on a clean sheet of waxed paper.
9. Brush a thin layer of rubber cement over the entire back of the heart.
10. Brush another thin layer of rubber cement over one side of another sheet of white paper. Cover the side completely.
11. Let the cement on both heart and paper dry.
12. Place the glued back of the heart in the center of the glued white paper. Press down flat.

LACY HEART

SCALLOP-EDGED

Ribbands were paper ribbons used as decorations in Polish homes and also took the place of ribbons on bridal wreaths. Ribband making is one of the oldest Polish paper-cutting crafts, and is still popular among the Polish citizens of America.

compass
colored paper
scissors

paste
tracing paper
pencil

1. Using the compass, draw a circle on a piece of colored paper.
2. Cut out the circle with a scissors, Fig. a.
3. Fold the circle in half, Fig. b. and in half again, Fig. c.
4. Fold the quarter-circle in half, Fig. d.
5. Cut a scalloped design in the outside edge of the folded circle. Make two small curved cuts in the sides of the folded circle near the point, Fig. e.
6. Unfold the circle.
7. Cut a curved design in the sides, and a zig-zag design into the bottom of two colored strips of paper, Fig. f.
8. Cut a larger curved design in the sides of two

more colored strips of paper cut a little smaller than the first two strips, Fig. g.
9. Paste the smaller strips to the center of the larger strips, Fig. h.
10. Paste each strip to the back of the scalloped circle, Fig. i.
11. Trace the feather pattern from the book (heavy solid and dotted outline) onto a sheet of tracing paper with a pencil.
12. Fold a piece of colored paper in half and transfer the pattern onto it, (see How to Transfer Patterns, page 20). Make sure to place the paper so that the dotted side of the pattern is on the folded edge of the paper, Fig. j.
13. Cut out the feather design. Following the above procedure, make another.
14. Paste a feather near the bottom of the front side of each ribbon. Paste a small triangle cut from another piece of colored paper under each feather.

RIBBANDS

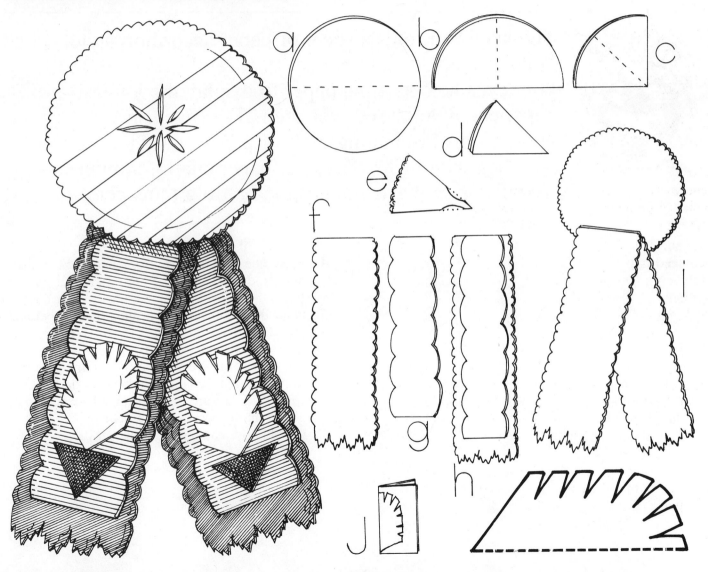

BATTLING RAMS

The magician folds a sheet of paper accordion-style. With a sharp scissors he makes several cuts. Before your eyes he opens the paper to display the longest paper chain you have ever seen. The Swedish brought this fascinating craft of paper-cutting to America with them. They cut paper chains composed of dolls or animals, such as the battling rams here.

scissors
colored paper
tracing paper
pencil

1. Cut a very long rectangular length out of colored paper. It should be as high as the ram pattern in the book.
2. Fold one end of the paper over. The fold should be as wide as the ground in the ram pattern.
3. Fold the paper back and forth, accordion-style, until all of the paper is used up, Fig. a.
4. Trace the ram pattern from the book (heavy solid and dotted outline) onto a sheet of tracing paper.
5. Place the pattern on top of the folded paper and transfer the design to it, Fig. b., (see How to Transfer Patterns, page 20).
6. Cut out the ram very carefully making sure you don't cut into the edges shown by a dotted line, Fig. c. Make sure to cut away all shaded areas shown in the pattern in the book.
7. Unfold your chain of battling rams.

ALL-IN-A-ROW

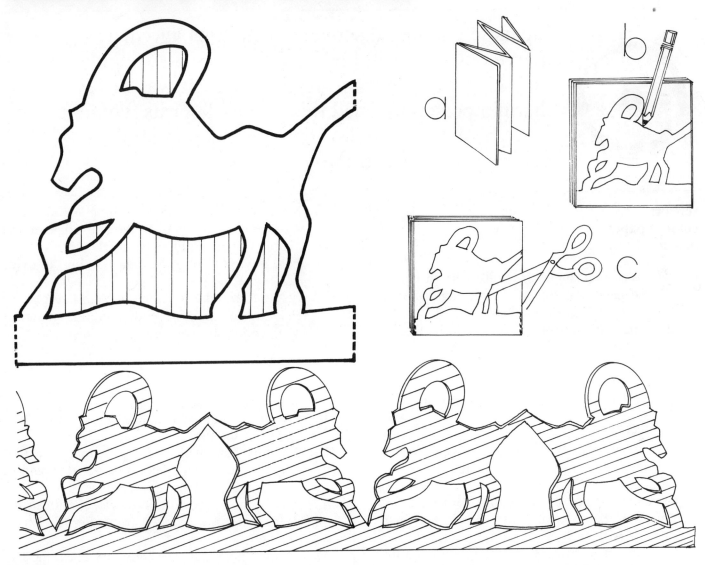

KAMI NINGYO

Japanese children discovered centuries ago that marvelous toys could be made of paper. A popular plaything was the Kami Ningyo doll. It was believed that if a person touched this doll evil spirits would leave his body. The doll, having taken in all the bad spirits, was then thrown in the river.

scissors   **string**
colored paper   **tape**
pencil

1. Cut out two rectangles from different sheets of colored paper the size of the rectangle shown around the doll in the drawing.
2. Place the two rectangles on top of each other.
3. Fold down the top of the rectangles to the place indicated by the single arrow in the drawing, and up to the place indicated by the double arrow. The paper should look like it does in Fig. a.
4. Turn the rectangles over, Fig. b.
5. With a pencil mark a point, Z, slightly to the left of the center of the folded edge. Mark the lefthand corner Y, see Fig. b.
6. Divide the side of the paper with Corner Y at its top into three equal parts. Mark the first division with an X, Fig. b.
7. Fold Corner Y down along the line formed by Points X and Z, Fig. c.

8. Mark the other top corner W. make an equal fold of Corner W over the top edge of the folded Corner Y, Figs. c. and d.
9. Fold the righthand side, side 1 in Fig. d, over, see Fig. e.
10. Fold out the bottom corner of Side 1, Fig. f.
11. Fold the lefthand side, Side 1 in Fig. f., almost to the opposite side, Fig. g.
12. Fold out the bottom corner of Side 2, Fig. h.
13. Wrap a strip of paper around the middle of the folded paper to make a waist, and tape it in place on the back.
14. Cut, roll, and tape a small piece of paper, Fig. i. This is the face.
15. Twist the bottom of the roll to form a neck, Fig. j.
16. Roll another small piece of paper. It should be slightly larger than the rolled face.
17. Tie the top of this roll into a gather with string, and cut out a window in front, Fig. k. This is the hair.
18. Slip the neck into the body and place the hair over the head, Fig. 1.

ORIGAMI DOLL

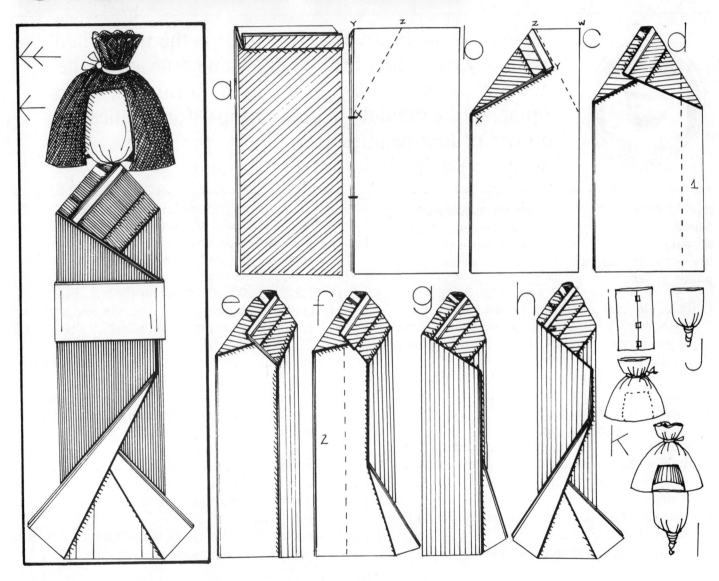

FOLDED DREIDEL

Chanukah is the Festival of Lights. It is the time when Jewish boys and girls receive gifts, one on each of the eight days of the holiday. A tradition during this season is spinning the dreidel—a kind of top—for pennies. You win or lose pennies according to the letter that shows on the dreidel after it is spun.

tracing paper
pencil
scissors
heavy paper (oaktag)
paper puncher

crayons or colored
  felt-tipped markers
liquid white glue
drinking straw

1. Trace the pattern for the dreidel (heavy solid and dotted outline) onto a sheet of tracing paper. The heavy lines are for cutting out on, and the dotted lines are for folding.
2. Cut out the tracing and place it on a piece of oaktag or heavy paper.
3. Trace around the pattern.
4. Cut out the dreidel shape.
5. With a crayon or colored felt-tipped marker, draw a letter on each center square shape as shown in the pattern in the book.
6. With a paper puncher, punch a hole through the square without any letters or dotted lines in it, see the book.
7. Fold the dreidel shape along all dotted lines (in one direction only), with letters facing out.
8. Fold the dreidel shape together to form a box with Tab W tucked inside, Fig. a.
9. Squeeze glue onto Tab W and press it to the inside of the box. Allow to dry.
10. Tuck Tabs X into the top of the box, Fig. b.
11. Fold the top side of the box, the one with the hole in it, over the folded tabs and glue down, Fig. c. Allow to dry.
12. Push the two points of the bottom triangles together with the Z flaps folded in, Fig. d.
13. Squeeze glue onto the Z flaps and push the remaining two triangles against them, Fig. e. All points should meet. Allow to dry.
14. Push half of a drinking straw into the hole at the top of the dreidel. The straw should go all the way to the point, Fig. f.
15. Squeeze glue around the straw where it enters the dreidel.
16. When the glue dries completely, spin the dreidel by the straw just as you do a top.

SPINNIING GAME

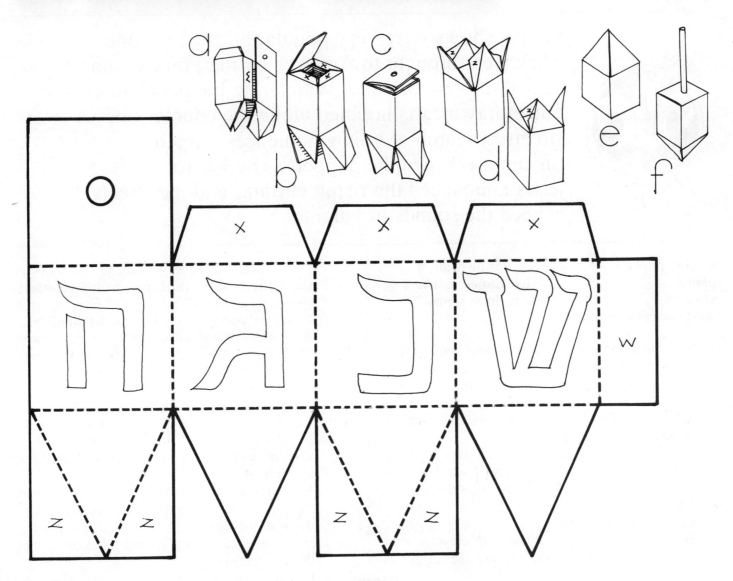

JOINTED PIERROT

Puppet shows were very popular all over Europe. They were brought to America by the French who settled in New Orleans. Wandering puppet shows on horse-drawn carts hobbled along the cobblestone streets in search of young audiences. A penny in a tin cup awakened the puppets. The Pierrot court jester announced the rising curtain, and the streets echoed the sounds of laughter.

tracing paper
pencil
scissors
white or colored paper

crayons or colored
felt-tipped markers
large dress snaps

1. Trace all of the patterns (heavy solid outlines) from the book onto a sheet of tracing paper.
2. Cut out each shape to use as a pattern.
3. Place the body pattern, Pattern A in the book, on a sheet of white or colored paper and trace around it.
4. Using the cutout patterns, trace two arms, Pattern B in the book, two upper legs, Pattern C, and two lower legs, Pattern D on the same paper.
5. Cut out all traced shapes.
6. Draw designs on each shape with crayons or colored felt-tipped markers. Follow the designs

in the book as a guide. Make sure you color on the correct sides of hands and feet—there should be a left and right in each pair, and that each hand and foot face in opposite directions.
7. With a sharpened pencil point or nail, twist small holes into the body, arms, top legs, and bottom legs at the X, Y, and Z points, as shown in the book patterns.
8. Open all of the snaps.
9. Attach each upper and lower leg together by pushing the inside of the snap through the two Z-holes, and then pressing the other half of the snap into it.
10. Attach the arms to the body at the X-points and the legs to the body at the Y-points just as you did with the legs.
11. Move the arms and legs to make the court jester do silly things.

COURT JESTER

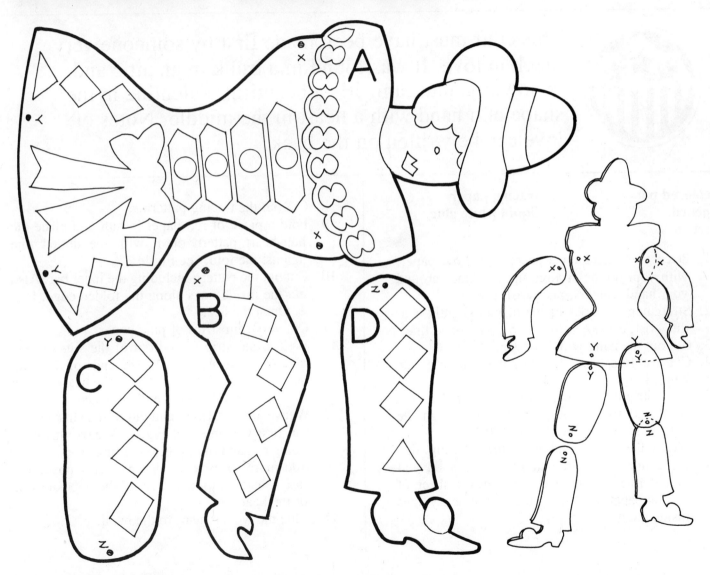

HEART-IN-HAND

This craft must have been made first by someone very much in love. It was found in a trunk in an attic and is now in a museum. It's a beautiful Valentine in the shape of a hand with a heart in the middle. Notes of love can be written on the back.

colored paper   tracing paper
pencil   liquid white glue
scissors

1. Place your hand on a sheet of yellow paper, with your thumb straight up, and trace around your hand, fingers, and wrist, Fig. a.
2. Straighten the sides of the tracing slightly near the wrist, as shown in Fig. b., see dotted line.
3. Cut out the hand with a scissors.
4. Cut evenly spaced slits near the bottom of the hand, Fig. c.
5. Cut a strip of pink paper that is longer than the wrist and wide enough to weave through the slits. Round the ends of the strip.
6. Weave the strip in and out of the slits, Fig. d.
7. Trace the half-heart pattern (heavy solid and dotted lines) from the book onto a sheet of tracing paper. Be sure to include all heavy lines inside the heart.
8. Cut out the tracing pattern.
9. Fold a piece of red paper in half and place the half-heart pattern on it with the dotted line against the fold, see Fig. e.
10. Cut out the pattern including the inner bar. Also cut the inside lines along the folded edge, Fig. e. Open the heart.
11. Cut very thin strips of pink paper.
12. Weave one strip in and out of the slits on one side of the heart, Fig. f. The ends of the strip should rest against the back of the heart. Add a dab of glue to hold the ends in place.
13. Weave a new strip in and out of the slits next to the first woven strip, Fig. g. Weave this strip going out and in opposite the first strip.
14. Add more strips, each one woven opposite the last. Continue until you reach the opposite side of the heart.
15. Glue the woven heart to the hand.

VALENTINE

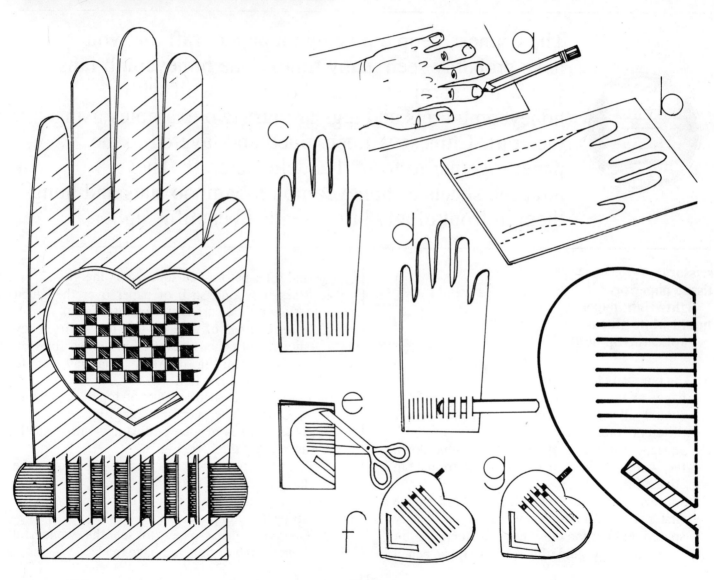

DELICATELY AIRY

The Chinese people invented a paper craft that you have probably seen many times. The honeycomb fans you win at carnivals or the bouncing wolf with honeycomb arms and legs are just two examples using the craft. Chinese women glued and layered tissue paper together to form this delicate craft. They attached sheets of honeycomb on bamboo slats and hung them in front of a light to create a beautiful sight

scissors
tissue paper or
   lightweight paper
liquid white glue in an
   applicator-tip bottle

1. Cut out many long strips of tissue or lightweight paper about half the size of this page. They should all be the same size. You can use different colors or all the same color.
2. Squeeze a thin line of liquid white glue down the width of the paper, a little in from both edges, Fig. a.
3. Squeeze more lines down the paper between the first two glue lines. They should be equally spaced and not too close to each other, Fig. b. You can draw guide-lines first with a pencil and ruler before you squeeze on the glue.
4. Place a second strip of paper over the glued strip with the corners matching, Fig. c.
5. Squeeze lines of glue on this new strip. They should fall exactly between the glued lines on the first strip, Fig. d. Again, you may want to draw guide-lines first.
6. Place another strip of paper on top of the second strip with the corners matching, Fig. e.
7. Squeeze lines of glue on this new strip exactly as you did the first, Fig. f.
8. Continue placing new strips of paper over the last glued strip as you did above.
9. Once you have glued your last strip, let all the strips dry completely.
10. Open the dried paper to see the wonderful honeycomb design you have made.

216

HONEYCOMB WINDOWS

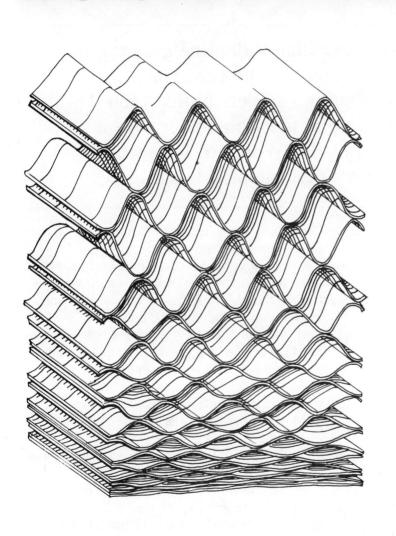

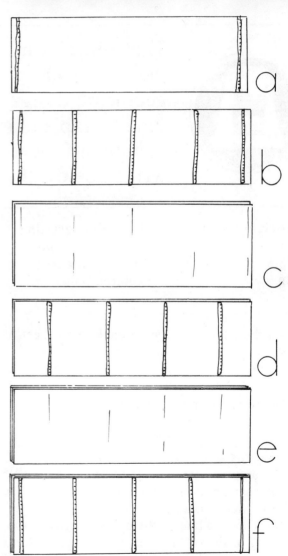

a

b

c

d

e

f

INTRICATE COBWEB

The cobweb card was a popular Valentine greeting in the early 1800's. In the center of the card was a geometric design like the kind spiders build when it's time to trap a dinner. Behind the web design was a picture of flowers or a person. Words of love were written below the web with its trapped design.

lightweight paper
compass
scissors
string

magazine, greeting
card or photo
liquid white glue
colored paper

1. With the compass, draw a circle on a sheet of lightweight paper about the size of a saucer.
2. Cut out the circle, Fig. a.
3. Fold the circle in half, Fig. b.
4. Fold the half-circle in half, Fig. c.
5. Fold the quarter circle in half, Fig. d.
6. Place the point of your compass at the tip of the folded circle, Point X in Fig. e.
7. Draw a curved line on the folded circle a little up from the bottom, Fig. e. Don't draw the line all the way across.
8. Draw a second line a little up from the first line, starting at the other side, Fig. f. Again, don't draw the line all the way across.

9. Continuing drawing lines across the quarter circle, almost to the very top, Fig. g.
10. Cut along all drawn lines. Be careful not to cut completely across the paper.
11. Unfold the paper and poke a small hole in the center with the point of the compass.
12. Push a length of string through the hole and tie a big knot on the back to hold it in place, Fig. h. The cobweb will open when the string is pulled, Fig. i.
13. Cut out a picture from a magazine or greeting card about the same size as the cobweb. You can also use a photograph.
14. Glue the picture to the center of a square piece of colored paper, Fig. j.
15. Squeeze glue on the outer rim of the cobweb on the same side that has the knot.
16. Glue the cobweb over the picture. Let it dry. When the string is pulled you will be able to see the picture through the cobweb.

PULL-OUT CARD

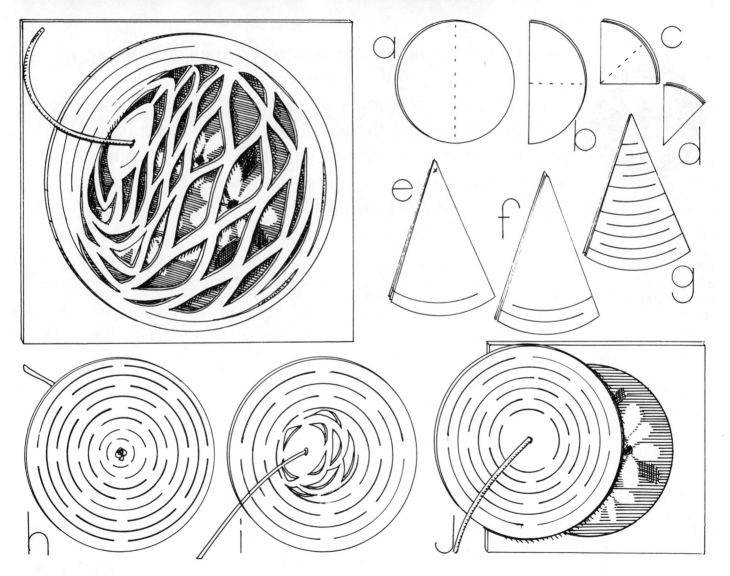

SUNDAY GOING-TO-

William H. Johnson was a famous black American painter. His style was quite primitive in design and color and in many ways resembles simple collage. He painted several thousand beautiful paintings. His style can be recreated with this colorful collage craft. The patterns for this project were taken from one of his prized paintings.

tracing paper
pencil
colored paper
scissors
paste

1. Trace all pattern shapes for the collage from the book onto a sheet of tracing paper. Be sure to include the part of the hill hidden by the cow's tail; and the part of the cart hidden behind the cow's tail.
2. Transfer each pattern piece onto a different sheet of colored paper, (see How to Transfer Patterns, page 20).
3. Cut out all designs with a scissors.
4. Paste each pattern on a sheet of paper following the drawing for placement.

CHURCH COLLAGE

COLORFUL FLOATING

Chinese homes in America were decorated with beautiful paper creations. Red was a popular color, and holidays were busy times for the paper cutters of the household. A feathery-looking paper fish made frequent appearances. It was cut from tissue paper and hung on the ceiling of the children's room. The fish was a sign of protection for the sleeping children.

tracing paper
pencil
smooth white paper
scissors

paper towel
glass of water
paintbrush
water color paints

1. Trace the goldfish (heavy solid outline) from the book onto a sheet of tracing paper with a pencil.
2. Place the tracing on top of a sheet of smooth white paper and transfer the drawing, (see How to Transfer Patterns, page 20).
3. Carefully cut out the fish. The dotted lines in the book illustration show you where to cut through the pattern to cut out the shaded areas.
4. Place the cut-out fish on a paper towel and brush water over the entire surface until it is very wet.
5. Quickly add water color paint to your paintbrush and dab the point of the brush on the wet paper. The color will spread by itself in the water on the paper.
6. Add dabs of red, yellow, and blue at different places on the fish. Be sure that you leave a lot of paper unpainted.
7. Let the water-painted fish dry flat.

PAPER=CUT FISH

WYCINANKI ROOSTER

Although this craft first appeared in the middle of the nineteenth century it has just recently emerged in America. Many Polish families have kept wycinanki alive, and one of the most popular designs is the rooster. He is shown in this craft surveying the world from the top of a fir tree.

tracing paper
pencil
colored paper
scissors
paste

1. With a pencil, trace the rooster, Pattern A; the wing, Pattern B, the tail designs, Patterns C and the tree design, Pattern D, from the book onto a sheet of tracing paper.
2. Place the rooster tracing on green or blue paper and transfer the design, (see How to Transfer Patterns, on page 20).
3. Transfer the wing and tail designs on light colored papers.
4. Transfer the tree design to a piece of folded red paper. Be sure to place the tracing paper on the folded paper so that the dotted side rests against the fold, Fig. a.
5. Cut out all designs, Fig. b.
6. Paste the wing and tail shapes to the bird.
7. Paste tree to a sheet of white paper and paste the bird sitting on top of it.

IN A FIR TREE

SILHOUETTES

Silhouettes were popular before the invention of the camera. It all started in France by a man whose name was Etienne de Silhouette. He loved to make paper-cut portraits in black or white paper.

white paper   **colored paper**
pencil   **paste**
scissors   **crayons or markers**

1. Have the person whose silhouette you want to draw sit in profile in front of you.
2. Draw an oval onto a neck, Fig. a.
3. Divide the lower half of the oval into three equal parts, Fig. b.
4. Carefully draw the outline of his or her head including hair and a collar, if any, on white paper, Fig. c. Cut out the head.
5. Trace around this head on black paper. Then cut out the head.
6. Paste the head on to the center of a sheet of white paper.
7. Cut colored paper to the size you wish your frame to be.
8. Cut out an oval in the center of the paper that is a little larger than the silhouette.
9. Decorate the frame with designs.
10. Paste the white paper to the back of the oval frame with the silhouette facing out of the oval.

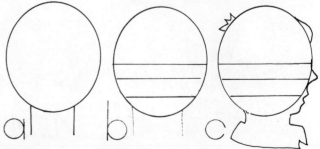

8

YARN

YARN

Skin and leather clothing was replaced when fabric
was invented. Fabric is made from woven fibers called
yarn. Besides fulfilling the most basic needs of people
for clothing, yarn has always played an important role
in craftwork. Yarn crafts were done by immigrant groups
from all countries in the world. These crafts were brought
to America to enrich the emerging national culture.

BIRDS-OF-A-FEATHER

 A Mexican yarn painting is a fiesta in color. Simple designs are worked into beautiful wall hangings. You won't need a paintbrush and jars of paint. Just a handful cf different colored yarn and you're on your way.

tracing paper　　**small paper cup**
pencil　　**paintbrush**
scissors　　**colored yarn**
cardboard　　**stick-on picture hanger**
liquid white glue

1. Trace the bird design from the book onto a sheet of tracing paper with a pencil. Include the dotted lines.
2. Cut a piece of cardboard as large as the box around the bird design.
3. Transfer the drawing onto the piece of cardboard, Fig. a (see How To Transfer Patterns, page 20).
4. Pour a little liquid white glue into a paper cup.
5. Paint in a petal of the flower with the glue and a paintbrush, Fig. b.

6. Lay the end of a piece of yarn over the drawn line, and press it into the glue, Fig. c.
7. Follow the line with yarn. Keep winding it into the area, Fig. d. The yarn should touch itself as you wind it into the glued area.
8. Fill in all areas of the flower and bird with glue and yarn.
9. Paint the areas marked X in the illustration with glue.
10. Wind a dark colored yarn into this background area.
11. Paint the remaining part of the background on the inner sides of the dotted line, with glue. Wind in a light yarn.
12. Add a stick-on picture hook to the back and hang.

YARN PAINTING

a

b

c

d

MOSAIC YARN

Ann Lee brought the Shaker community to America in 1774. Shakers settled in Niskeyuna, New York, and gradually moved into Ohio, Indiana, and Kentucky. The Shakers were a religious sect that believed in communal life and great self-discipline. They designed and built some of the finest and simplest furniture and home utensils America has ever seen.

burlap or heavy fabric
scissors
tracing paper
pencil

carbon paper
liquid white glue in
   an applicator-tip bottle
yarn

1. Cut a piece of burlap or heavy fabric larger than the design in the book.
2. Trace the design from the book onto a sheet of tracing paper with a pencil.
3. Place the carbon side of a sheet of carbon paper onto the burlap or fabric.
4. Place the tracing over the carbon paper.
5. Carefully draw over the lines of the tracing. Try to draw with the side of the pencil rather than with the point, Fig. a.
6. Remove the carbon paper and the tracing.

7. Fold over one edge of the burlap or fabric and glue it down for a hem.
8. Hem the remaining three sides, Fig. b. Glue down all hems.
9. Squeeze liquid white glue from an applicator-tip bottle along the line of one flower petal, Fig. c.
10. Lay the end of a piece of yarn on the glued line and follow the outline with the yarn.
11. Squeeze glue into the petal area and fill with yarn (see Birds-Of-A-Feather Yarn Painting, page 230). Cut away the yarn when area is filled.
12. Fill in all other areas of the design with yarn.
13. Fill in the background. To make a larger rug, make many more small rugs and have one of your parents help you sew them together.

SHAKER RUG

FLUFFY POM-POM

If you were a Mexican merchant selling your wares on a donkey cart, you would want everyone do know you were coming. In Southern California and parts of Texas, Mexican salesmen added bells to their donkey pulls to announce their arrival. The bell pulls were made of yarn and gaily decorated just like the one you are about to make. Since you probably don't have a burro, hang them in your room.

yarn
cardboard
scissors

1. Tie the ends of three very long pieces of yarn together, Fig. a.
2. Bring the lefthand strand marked X in Fig. a, over the middle strand, Fig. b.
3. Bring the righthand strand, marked Y, over the middle strand, Fig. c.
4. Continue braiding strands, first left and then right over the middle strand, until you reach the bottom of the three strands of yarn, Fig. d.

5. Tie the ends together at the bottom of the braid.
6. Cut a medium-sized square out of cardboard.
7. Wrap yarn forty times around the piece of cardboard, Fig. e.
8. Tie all of the yarn together at the center on both sides of the cardboard, Fig. f.
9. Cut the wrapped yarn at the top and bottom of the cardboard, Figs. g and h.
10. Pull apart the yarn to fluff the two tied bundles of yarn into pom-poms, Fig. i.
11. Wrap two more different colored yarns around the cardboard and make four more pom-poms.
12. Tie three different colored pom-poms to each end of the braid.

DONKEY PULL

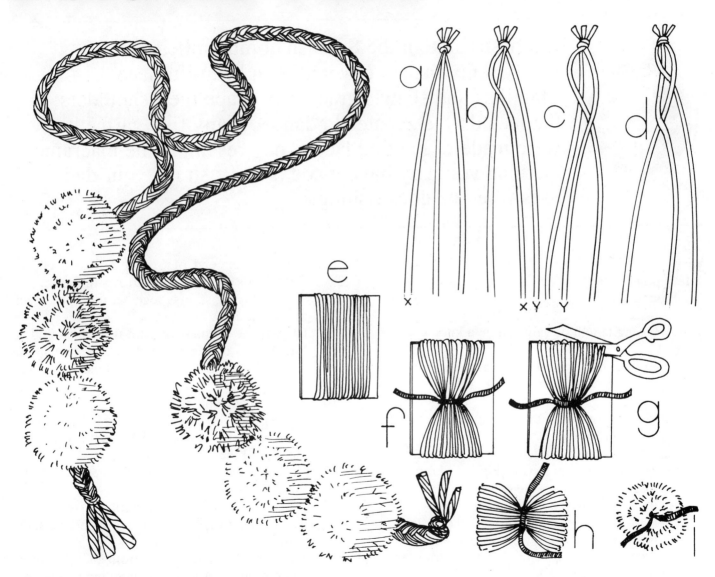

a
b
c
d

e

f

g

h

x
x Y Y

235

HANGING "FISH NET"

It's fiesta time in the Spanish communities and the lovely señoritas are covered with beautiful lace. Mantillas and shawls gracefully drape their shoulders; the men do the zapateado dance. Many fine garments were made of knotted lace. They resemble the macramé clothing you may have made or the fish net your dad uses when he goes fishing.

scissors
yarn
safety pins
cardboard

1. Cut a long length of yarn and tie a knot at each end.
**2. Carefully pin the yarn tightly across the top of a large piece of cardboard. Pin through the knots, Fig. a.
3. Cut several long strands of yarn. The drawing shows seven strands.
4. Hang each strand doubled over the yarn pinned to the top of the cardboard, Fig. a. Make sure the ends of the strands are even.
5. Tie the strands to the pinned yarn, Fig. b.
6. To start lacing, tie one end of the lefthand strand, Strand 1 in Fig. c., to one end of its neighbor, Strand 2, slightly down from the pinned strand, Fig. c.

7. Tie the other end of Strand 2 to one end of Strand 3 as shown by the arrows in Fig. c.
8. Continue tying strands together until you reach the last strand.
9. To start the second row, tie the untied end of Strand 1 to one of the ends of the new strand formed by tying Strand 1 and Strand 2 together, Fig. d.
10. Tie the other end of the new strand (Strand 1 plus 2) with the next hanging end.
11. Continue tying ends together until you have completed the second row.
12. Make the third row following the same directions for the very first row.
13. Continuing making rows until you reach the desired length you want. There should be some yarn hanging at the bottom.
14. Remove the knotted lace from the cardboard and pin, glue, or sew it to anything you want.

KNOTTED LACE

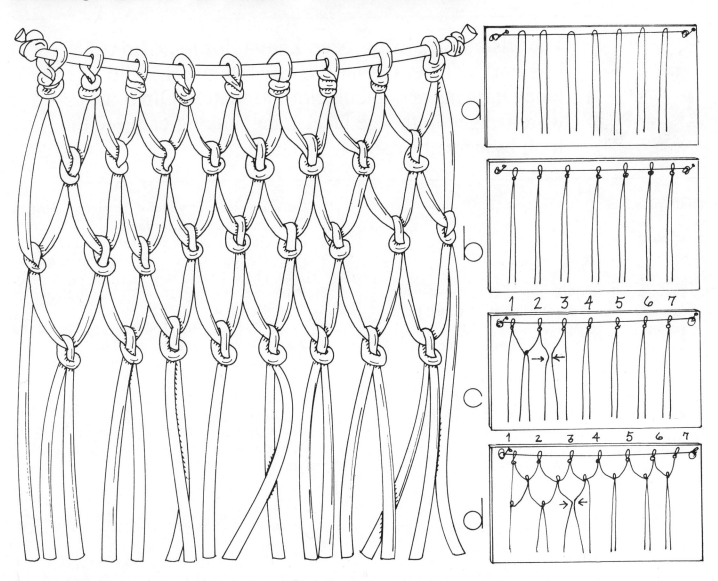

KNOTTED FRINGED

The Irish have always been known for their fine lacework. There was nary an Irish home that didn't have fancy napkins and a tablecloth to match. Often they were fringed with fine lace. Lace making came to the Irish by way of Spain.

safety pins
yarn
cardboard
scissors

**1. Pin a length of yarn to a piece of cardboard just as you did in the "Fish Net" Knotted Lace project in this chapter.
2. Tie strands of yarn doubled over to the pinned yarn, Fig. a.
3. Tie the first two rows of lace as described in the "Fish Net" Knotted Lace in this chapter. Leave smaller spaces between the rows, Fig. b.
4. Tie the remaining rows just as you did the first two rows making larger spaces between rows. Fig. c.

5. Cut short pieces of yarn for the pieces of fringe. They can be different colors.
6. Fold one of those pieces of yarn in half, Fig. d.
7. Place the folded loop over a section of knotted lace, Fig. e.
8. Bring the hanging ends up and through the loop, Fig. f.
9. Pull the ends tightly. The front and back of the knot will look like Figs. g and h.
10. Knot as many pieces of yarn on the knotted lace as you desire.
11. Tie the hanging bottom ends of each yarn fringe together.
12. Remove the knotted fringed lace from the cardboard and pin, glue, or sew it to anything you want.

FANCY LACE

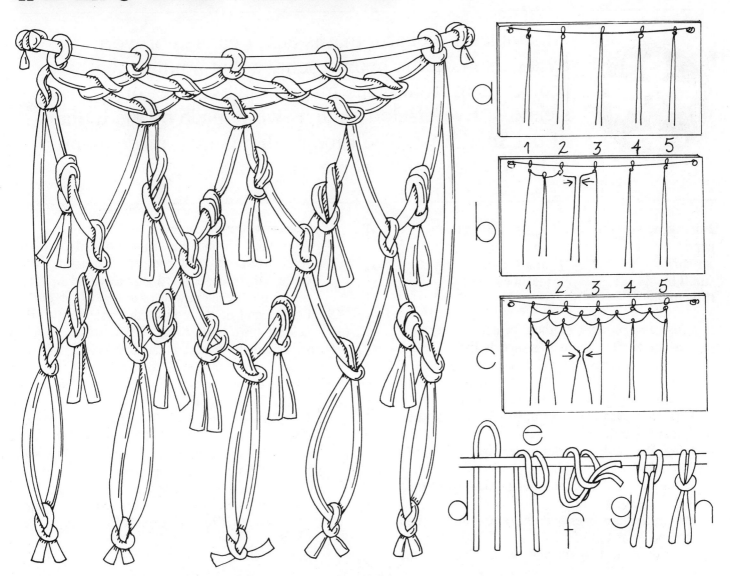

239

EYE OF GOD

An amulet is a charm that is either carried or worn by a person. Some people believe that amulets will protect them from black magic, the evil eye, or sickness. Eye-of-God amulets were made by the Indians of the Southwest. The tribe medicine man made them to be worn by tribespeople who were sick.

2 drinking straws
yarn
scissors
small beads
thin string

liquid white glue
waxed paper
small shells
feather

1. Cross two straws at their centers to form a perfect X. Tie them together at the crossing point with a long length of yarn, Fig. a.
2. With the knot at the back, bring the yarn behind the upper righthand arm marked Arm 1 in Fig. b.
3. Bring the yarn over and under Arm 1 and then behind Arm 2, Fig. c.
4. Bring the yarn over and under Arm 2 and then behind Arm 3, Fig. d.
5. Bring the yarn over and under Arm 3 and then behind Arm 4, Fig. e.
6. Bring the yarn over and under Arm 4 and then behind Arm 1, Fig. f.
7. Start at Arm 1 again and begin wrapping the yarn as you did before.
8. Wrap yarn around the arms until only a small section of each straw end remains visible. You can use different colored yarn as you wrap. Just tie the end of the new yarn to that of the old.
9. Tie the end of the end of the wrapping to the nearest straw end.
10. String small beads on a small piece of thin string. Tie both ends of the string to two adjacent straw ends, see illustration. Add a dab of glue to the knots.
11. String a long length of thin string with beads, and tie the ends to the two remaining straw ends. Add a dab of glue to the knots. You will hang the amulet from this strand.
12. Lay the amulet on a sheet of waxed paper and glue tiny shells to the shorter string of beads. Glue a feather to one corner of the "eye," see illustration.
13. Hang when dry.

WARRIOR AMULET

OJO DE DIOS

There are two cultures that made the hypnotizing Ojo de Dios or Eye of God: the Indian and the Mexican. This craft came to America from Mexico. It has a center eye and smaller eyes at the top and sides. It was the custom in Mexican families to add an eye every time a child was born. After the fourth child, a new Eye of God was made or another eye added where there was space. The Ojo de Dios became a family tree.

3 drinking straws
stapler
scissors
colored yarn
cardboard

1. Place two drinking straws on top of each other, forming a perfect cross, and staple them together, Fig. a.
2. Cut the third straw into three equal pieces.
3. Place each straw section across each of the two side arms and across the top arm, Fig. b. Staple in place. Make sure the arms of these smaller crosses are all equal.
4. Wrap the crossed center straws with different colored yarns just as you did in the Eye Of God Amulet in this chapter. Wrap only halfway toward the side and top crosses, Fig. c.
5. Wrap each side and top cross just as you did the center cross, Fig. d.
6. Cut a small rectangle from a piece of cardboard with scissors.
7. Wrap yarn around the cardboard four times, Fig. e.
8. Tie the wrapped yarn in the middle on both sides of the cardboard, Fig. f.
9. Cut the yarn away from the cardboard at the top and bottom of the cardboard, Fig. g.
10. Tie the gathered yarn to one arm of the outer crossed arms of the Eye of God, Fig. h.
11. Make enough gathers for all of the arms and tie them on.

BIRTHDAY MARKER

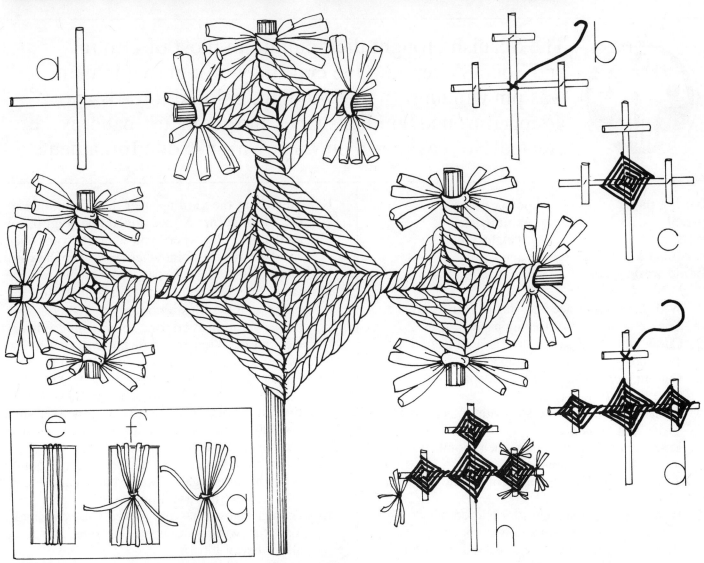

WRAPPED YARN=STAR

The Spanish brought their culture to most of Central and South America. One craft they brought with them was pin winding. In pin winding, colored threads are wrapped around familiar shapes and geometric patterns are created. Holidays had their very own pin-wound ornaments.

tracing paper
pencil
scissors
cardboard
liquid white glue

poster paints
paintbrush
straight pins
yarn

1. With a pencil, trace the star pattern from the book onto a sheet of tracing paper.
2. Cut out the tracing and use it as a guide to draw two stars on a piece of cardboard.
3. Cut out the two stars with a scissors.
4. Glue the two stars together.
5. Paint both sides of the star with poster paints, or leave it unpainted.
**6. Push a straight pin into each point. Leave some of the pin extending.
7. Tape the end of a long length of yarn to the back of the star.
8. Bring the yarn over the top right corner of the star that is marked with an X in Fig. a.
9. Bring the yarn over and behind the fourth corner marked with a Y, Fig. a.
10. Now bring the yarn up over the next corner to the left of corner X, see dotted line, Fig. b. (X marks the point where you wrap the yarn over and Y marks the point where you wrap the yarn under. You always bypass three points.)
11. Study Fig. c. You will notice that, for the purpose of the illustration, all numbered points have been moved one position counter-clockwise. Wrap the yarn up around the new corner Y and up over the corner left of the new corner X, see dotted line, Fig. c. You will continue to wrap up around each new Y and over the corner to the left or each new X until you have done one complete wrapping around the star, Figs. c through i.
12. When you have reached the starting point, begin all over again, fitting the second wrapping next to the first, Fig. j.
13. The star shown has only three yarn windings. You can wind yarn up to the pins, covering all of the cardboard.
14. Tie the end of the yarn to a pin. Hang your star.

PIN WINDING

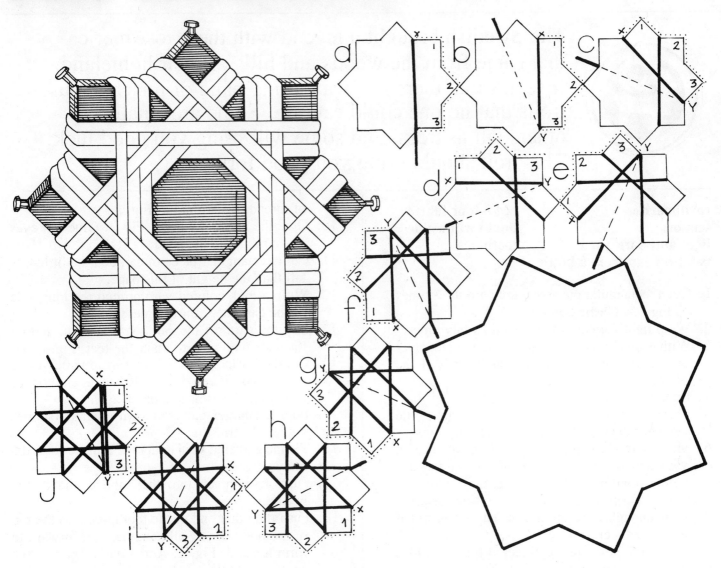

GOOD FORTUNE

The Swedish brought a legend with them to America that came from the woods and hills of their homeland. It seems that there is a wandering band of mischievous trolls that no one could capture. Some are small, others tall as trees, and some will bring you good luck. This troll should bring you good fortune.

cardboard
scissors
light and dark yarn
twist-off cap from a bottle

red felt or fabric
liquid white glue
toothpick

1. Cut a rectangular piece of cardboard three times as big as a plastic bottle cap.
2. Wrap light yarn around the card twenty times.
3. With a small piece of yarn, tie the yarn together at the top of the cardboard and cut it at the bottom, Fig. a.
4. Remove the yarn from the cardboard, Fig. b.
5. Place the knotted yarn over the plastic bottle cap with the top of the cap facing you, Fig. c.
6. Make sure the cap is completely covered with yarn and tie the yarn together under the cap with a small piece of yarn, Fig. d.
7. Cut a long piece of red felt or fabric for a hat wide enough to fit around the cap when rolled into a cylinder.
8. Glue the fabric into a cylinder at the back, Fig.e.
9. When dry, gather the hat at the top with a piece

of thread tied around it, Fig. e.
10. Glue the hat to the head, Fig. f. Glue felt eyes and a mouth to the head.
11. Cut a rectangular piece of cardboard a little less tall than the height of this page.
12. Wrap a dark colored yarn around the long side of the cardboard thirty times, Fig. g.
13. Slip the yarn off the cardboard, Fig. h, and tie the ends with yarn to make the feet, Fig. i.
14. Cut the cardboard in half and wrap yarn around one piece fifteen times. Remove and tie as above for the arms and hands.
15. Fold the larger gathered yarn over the shorter gathered yarn, Fig. j.
16. Tie the gathered yarn under the arms to form the body, Fig. k.
17. Push a toothpick into the knotted end of the head.
18. Push the other end of the toothpick into the top of the body. Bring all hanging yarn forward to form a beard, Fig. 1. Add a dab of glue to the neck to hold the head in place.

TROLL DOLL

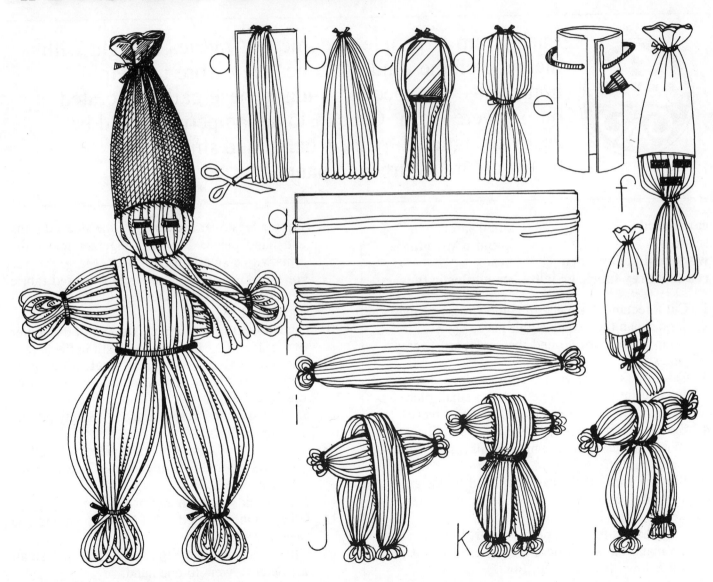

247

BALLOON SLEEVE

Each group of people to come to America brought with them the clothes and costumes they wore in their homelands. On special holidays these gaily decorated outfits were worn. Czechoslovakian people could be easily recognized by their ballooned shirts and bright-colored skirts and pants.

cardboard
scissors
white and yellow yarn
red and grey fabric or felt

small safety pin
liquid white glue
beads
small plastic flowers

1. Cut a rectangular piece of cardboard two times larger than the height of this page.
2. Wrap white yarn around the cardboard twenty times, Fig. a.
3. Carefully slip the yarn off the cardboard, Fig. b., and tie the ends together with small pieces of yarn, Fig. c. This is the leg and feet piece.
4. Cut the cardboard in half (see arrows in Fig. a). Wrap white yarn around on this piece forty times.
5. Slip the yarn off the cardboard and tie the ends to make the hands. Also tie the yarn at the center, Fig. d.
6. Fold the wrapped leg piece in half, Fig. e.
7. To make the head, tie the leg piece together a little down from the top, Fig. f.

8. Slip the legs over the center of the sleeved arms and hand piece. Tie them together under the arms with a small piece of yarn, Fig. g.
9. For the skirt, cut a large circle from red fabric or felt. Cut around the ege of the circle as shown in Fig. h.
10. Cut a hole, the size of a nickle, out of the center of the skirt, Fig. h. Cut a small slit in the hole.
11. For the vest, cut a long rectangle from grey fabric or felt. Cut an oval hole in the center of the vest, Fig. i.
12. Slip the skirt and vest on the doll. Safety pin the skirt to the back.
13. Make a little bundle of long pieces of yellow yarn and tie together at centers. Glue it to the top of the head, Fig. j.
14. Make braids on each end of the hair, Fig. j.
15. Glue a piece of red fabric or felt around the head for a hat.
16. Glue bead eyes to the head and tie small artificial flowers to one hand.

COSTUME DOLL

CHIEF'S WOVEN

The Indians' sense of beauty can be seen in the weavings they did. Blankets were woven with yarns dipped in natural dyes. Their designs included religious and nature symbols. The Navahos were the best weavers of the Indian Nation. The woven hanging you make should contain your own favorite colors.

scissors
large piece of cardboard
ruler
pencil
yarn

beads
liquid white glue
paper towel tube
feathers

1. Cut a piece of cardboard as wide as this page and as long as you desire.
2. Use a ruler to draw a rectangle within the larger cardboard piece, Fig. a.
**3. Cut out the middle rectangle with a scissors, Fig. a.
**4. Cut an even number of small slits on the top and bottom edges fairly close together, Fig. a.
5. Knot one end of a long length of yarn and slip the knotted end into the first slit on the left at the bottom of the loom.
6. Bring the yarn up to the first slit on the top left, over to the next top slit, and then down to the second slit on the bottom.
7. Keep wrapping yarn tightly up and down, going into all slits, Fig. b.
8. Tie the end of the yarn into the last slit on the

bottom right of the loom.
9. Tie the end of a piece of yarn to the first lefthand strand of yarn on the frame, quite a bit down from the top. See the top arrow in Fig. c.
10. Pass the yarn over and under the lengths of yarn on the frame.
11. When you reach the last length of yarn on the right, bring the yarn around it, and weave the second row in and out, going in where you went out, out where you went in on the first row. Weave loosely. Tie on new yarn in new colors as you weave.
12. Stop weaving a little bit up from the bottom. See the bottom arrow in Fig. c.
13. Slip the weaving off the frame and cut the bottom loops.
14. To make the bottom fringe, tie every two yarn ends together at the top and bottom with beads strung between the two knots, Fig. d.
15. Slip a paper towel tube through the top loops, Fig. d.
16. Glue feathers to the weaving.
17. Tie yarn to both ends of the tube and hang.

HANGING

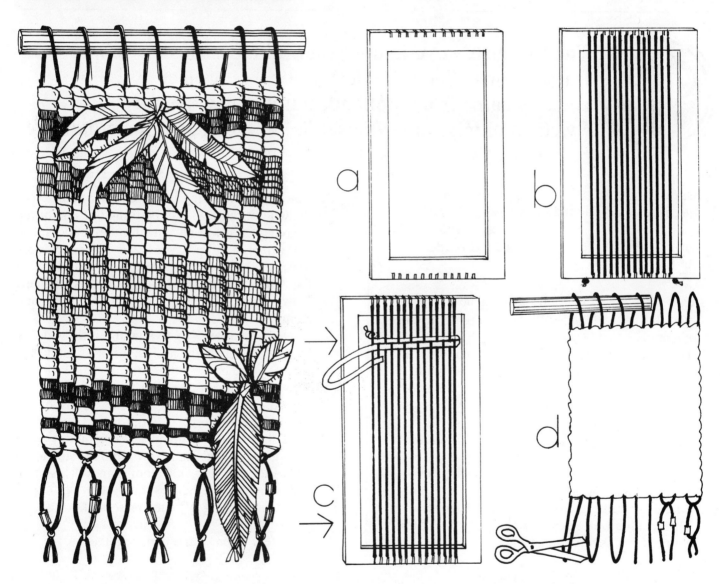

a

b

c

d

251

COLORFUL WOVEN

 The Swedish wove many beautiful tapestries on simple frame looms. The tulip design for this project actually came from Holland, but it was woven by Swedish immigrants who settled in the New Amsterdam area.

scissors   colored yarn
large piece of cardboard   stapler
pencil   canvas needle
ruler   needle threader
paste

**1. Cut out a weaving frame and thread it just as you did in the Chief's Woven Hanging in this chapter.

2. Trace the tulip design (all three tulips) from the book onto a sheet of tracing paper with a pencil.

3. Cut a second piece of cardboard exactly the same size as the frame.

4. Paste the tracing onto the center of this piece of cardboard.

5. Place the cardboard with the tracing on it behind the frame in line with it, Fig. a.

6. Staple the frame and design-cardboard together.

7. Thread a canvas needle with a length of pink yarn. Use a needle threader.

8. You will be weaving in areas rather than across the whole frame. Begin by tying one end of the weaving yarn to one yarn on the frame at the top tip of a tulip. Weave in the entire area loosely, following the design as described in the Chief's Woven Hanging in this chapter. Now weave the areas over the leaves and stems.

9. Tie yarn to an end loom strand a little ways up from the top of the tulips, Fig. b., and start weaving the background.

10. When you reach the top point of the tulip, thread the needle into the side loops of the tulip-weaving, Fig. c. Continue weaving the background in this manner. Remember that all background weaving is sewn into the side loops of the flower, leaf, and stem shapes. This holds the weaving together.

11. Slip the weaving off the frame and cut all the loops.

12. Tie every three strand ends together.

TULIP TAPESTRY

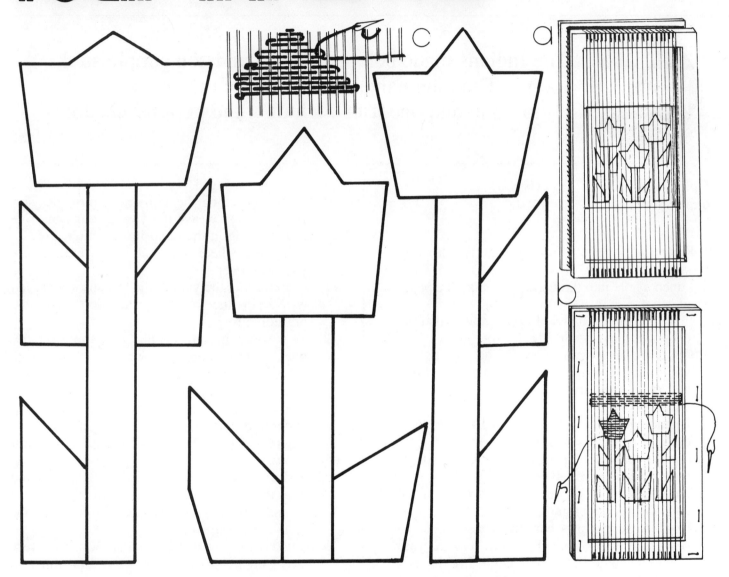

STICK WEAVE

The Indians made belts and headbands on simple stick looms. The long bands of thin fabric thus created had a thousand and one uses including the popular headband.

5 plastic straws   **scissors**
paper puncher   **yarn**

1. Pinch flat one end of each of the five drinking straws.
2. Punch a hole into the flattened end with a paper puncher, Fig. a.
3. Pinch the punched end of each straw so that the ends are round again, Fig. b.
4. Cut five long pieces of yarn. The yarn should wrap around your waist three times for a belt and two times around your head for a headband.
5. Thread each piece of yarn through the hole in each of the straws, Fig. c.
6. Fix the yarn on each straw so that both ends of each piece of yarn fall equally, Fig. d.
7. Tie a long piece of yarn to one straw near the end. Do not tie it tightly, Fig. e.
8. Hold the five straws parallel to each other, at one end, in your hand. The straw with the yarn tied to it should be on the bottom, Fig. f.
9. To weave, wrap the yarn under then over all five straws, Fig. f.
10. When you reach the top straw, turn the yarn around it and weave the yarn through the five straws going in the opposite direction, Fig. f., going over where you went under, under where you went over.
11. Keep turning the yarn at the last straw and then weave in the opposite direction than the preceding row.
12. As the weaving grows, pull the straws one by one, until the weaving moves onto the hanging yarn. Tie more yarn of a different color to the weaving-yarn as necessary.
13. Stop weaving when you have made a belt long enough to fit around your waist or head.
14. Tie the end of the weaving-yarn to the last straw.
15. Push the last of the weaving off the straws and onto the hanging yarn. Keep pulling the straws so that the hanging yarn on both sides of the weaving are equal in length.
16. Cut the yarn away from the straws. Tie every two hanging strands together several times to form a large knot.

A BELT OR BAND

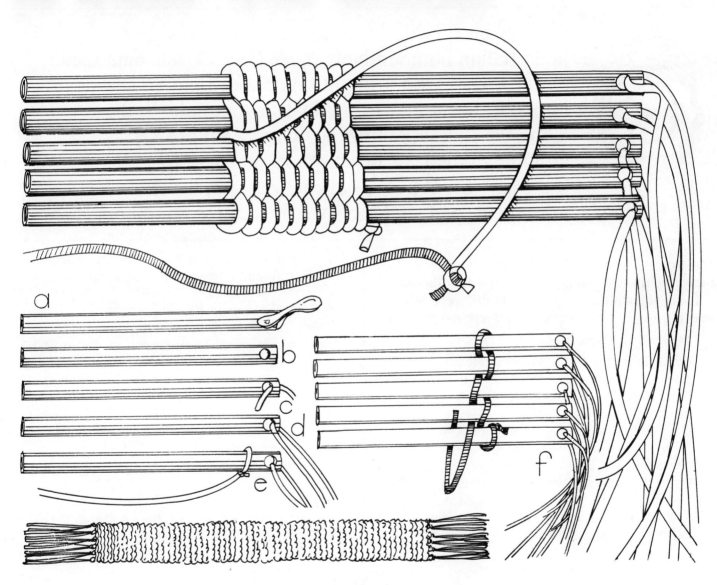

a

b

c

d

e

f

CROSS-STITCH

The design for this cross stitch project was found in an Italian home in New York City. It was handmade by the owner who brought this craft to America with him. The scene, a sailing boat, is a popular sight along the Italian Peninsula. Italian families felt at home in the East because the seacoast was close by. Many brought the delicate art of cross stitching with them, and sold their wares to local neighbors.

scissors
fabric lightweight enough
   to see through
pencil

embroidery hoop
embroidery thread
   in different colors
wide-eye needle

1. Cut a piece of lightweight fabric larger than this page. You can use a colored fabric if you like.
2. Place the fabric over the cross-stitch boat in this book.
3. Carefully trace all of the X marks onto the fabric with a soft pencil. You can also use a yellow felt-tipped marker.
4. Open an embroidery hoop and place one half under the cross stitch design. Place the other half over the fabric, push one hoop into the other while pulling the fabric tightly.

**5. Knot one end of a long length of embroidery thread and thread the other end through a wide-eye needle.
6. The four dots in Fig. a represent the four ends of an X. Push the needle up through an X in the fabric at the end which corresponds to End 1, Fig. a.
7. Bring the needle over and down through End 2, then up and out through End 3, Fig. b.
8. Bring the needle over to End 4, Fig. c. Push the needle through it, then over to a new End 1 on the next X. Repeat Steps 6, 7, and 8.
9. Cross stitch the entire design using different colors for different parts.
10. Fold an edge of fabric back and sew it down with cross stitches. Do the same with the other edges to make a cross-stitch hem.

SAILING BOAT

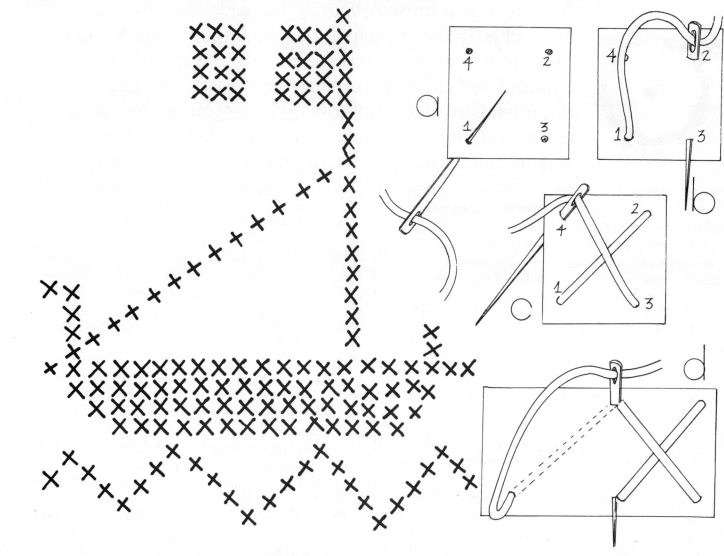

257

SPOT-EMBROIDERED

A kimono is a loose robe that has wide sleeves and is worn chiefly by women. Japanese kimonos were and are made of the finest materials and are frequently embroidered. Maybe you have seen the fiery dragons or garlands of lotus blossoms which were embroidered on the old kimonos. Now your home can have the elegant touch of Japan when you complete this project.

scissors
lightweight white fabric
liquid white glue in
  an applicator-tip bottle
waxed paper
colored felt-tipped
  markers
embroidery hoop
wide-eye needle
embroidery thread

1. Cut out a piece of lightweight, white fabric larger than this page.
2. Fold over all edges of the fabric and glue them down.
3. Place a sheet of waxed paper over the flower drawing in the book. This will protect the book when you color the fabric.
4. Place the fabric over the waxed paper.
5. Color in the design on the fabric with felt-tipped markers. Make the flowers yellow and the leaves different shades of green.
6. Remove the fabric and the waxed paper from the book.
7. Open an embroidery hoop and place one half of the hoop under the flower design, the other half over it.
8. Push one hoop into the other while pulling the fabric tightly, Fig. a.
**9. Thread a wide-eye needle with embroidery thread. The color of the thread should match the color of the section you are going to embroider.
10. Bring the needle up and through one end of a section of the design, Fig. b.
11. Bring the needle over and back down on the line of the opposite side of the design, Fig. c.
12. Bring the needle back up and through the outline, across, and back down, Fig. d.
13. Continue filling in sections of the design with the appropriate color of embroidery thread for each section.
14. Cut all thread ends on the underside of the fabric.
15. Leave some sections of the flower design without embroidery. Remove embroidery from hoop and hang or display as you wish.

FLOWERS AND LEAVES

a

b

c

d

e

259

ROLLED STRING BALL

The Chinese who settled in California used to make string balls for their children. It was really an art since they embroidered designs on the outer strings.

saved string
wide-eye needle
colored yarn

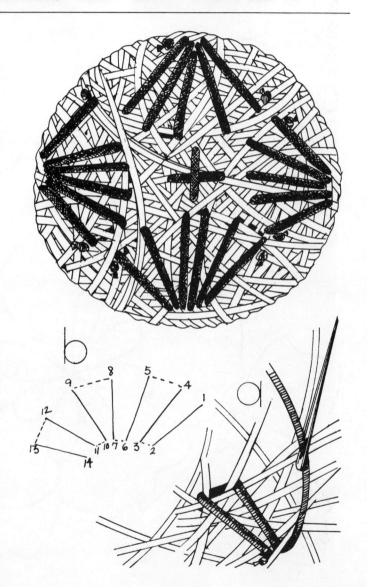

1. Roll the largest length of string around itself and into a tight ball.
2. Tie another piece of string to the end of the rolled string and continue rolling.
3. Keep tying and rolling string onto the ball. Make the ball the size of a tennis ball.
4. Tie the end of the last wrapped string to a string on the ball.
**5. Thread a wide-eye needle with yarn.
6. Embroider a design on the ball sewing through the wrapped string, Fig. a.
7. To make the fan design, first study Fig. b. All stitches are made by sewing in and up, over, down. The dotted lines in Fig. b. indicate where the yarn is stitched under the wrapped string.
8. Tie the end of the embroidered fan to a string on the ball.

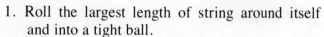

9

BAZAAR

BAZAAR

A bazaar is a kind of fair where games of chance
are played, tasty foods are eaten, and items
are sold, usually to benefit a charity or an
organization. Now, with the help of your friends
or group, you can plan a heritage tree
bazaar to sell craft projects made from this book.

PLANNING A HERITAGE TREE CRAFT BAZAAR FOR TEN OR MORE PARTICIPANTS

THINGS FOR ADULTS TO DO

There are many things an adult must do to make a children's craft bazaar a reality. The bazaar is a large undertaking which will require an investment of your time, including a little roadwork. When you see the smiles on your children's faces, however, and their hands at work, you will know your hard work was well worth the effort. Below is a checklist of preliminary things that have to be done once you and your children decide to run a bazaar. The actual preparation for the bazaar begins once the following have been arranged.

ADULT'S CHECKLIST

• Discuss with the children who will run the bazaar and who will receive the proceeds from it. It is best to place the project under the auspices of a group: the Boy Scout, Girl Scout, Cub Scout, or Brownie troop, Little League team, Sunday school or grade-school class. Of course, the bazaar may be put together by a group no more official than a bunch of neighborhood friends.

• You will have to find a place for the bazaar; church hall, school auditorium, gymnasium, on the block, backyard, etc. Just about any reasonably sized space should do.

• You will have to choose a date on which the bazaar will be held, and a rain date if it is to be held outdoors. Decide at what time the bazaar will open and close as well.

• The bazaar should be advertised. You can help your children with the advertising in many ways. They will be making announcements or fliers which will have to be duplicated. If you have access to a duplicating, mimeograph, or Xerox machine, this could be a great help. You will have to organize a meeting just for making posters and announcements. You might get in touch with local radio stations which announce community events and ask to have the bazaar mentioned on the air. Newspapers are frequently willing to give copy space for local news items. You may belong to church groups or other organizations which would be willing to advertise your children's bazaar, especially if it is to be for a worthy cause.

• Supervision of the planning, and of the bazaar itself is very important. Don't try to do it alone. Get several adults together to chaperone all aspects of the bazaar. One or two adults should be present at every planning meeting.

• After the bazaar is over, see to it that the children take down all booths, etc., and clean up the site. The site should be returned to a state as neat and clean as it was prior to the bazaar. All borrowed furniture and accessories should be returned to their owners.

• The children should turn over all proceeds to you or another designated adult. Children who contributed money for supplies should be reimbursed. The remaining money should be changed into a money order or a personal check made out to the charity or organization which is to receive the proceeds. The last page of this book has a gift acknowledgement on it that should be copied, filled out, and sent to the recipient of the money.

THINGS FOR CHILDREN TO DO

You want your craft bazaar to be a great success and this will require some organizing. First of all, you will have to choose who—or what group—will run it, and who will receive the proceeeds you will collect. Will your Boy Scout, Girl Scout, Brownie or Cub Scout troop run the bazaar? Or what about making it a project of your Sunday school class, Little League team, or grade-school class? Any group of friends can put on a bazaar—just get the neighborhood kids together. Have all the adults who lead your group or the appropriate parents help you. The more people in on the bazaar, the better.

There are many things you and your group must do to get the bazaar ready. You should have at least four planning meetings. On the following pages you

will find the agenda (things to do) for all the meetings, and when to hold them in relation to the bazaar's opening date. If you cover the agenda for each meeting thoroughly, your bazaar should be a great success. It will take at least six weeks to complete all preparations. Your chaperones will have made all the necessary preliminary arrangements—where, when and what time the bazaar will be held—before your first meeting. Then the bazaar truly becomes a joint effort.

MEETINGS AND THEIR AGENDAS

MEETING 1—1st Week

Old Business

Your adult organizers will tell you and your group where the bazaar will be held, the date and the rain date (if necessary), and what time it will begin and end.

New Business

Your group should look through the book and decide which crafts it will want to make and sell, and how many of each craft will be needed. Make each person responsible for making one of the crafts, as many as will be needed. You should allow the whole group two weeks to complete all crafts.

MEETING 2—3rd Week

Old Business

All completed crafts should be accounted for and on hand for display.

New Business

1. Decide how much to charge for each craft. An easy way to determine this is to add up how much it costs to make each craft and double that cost.

2. Make paper price tags and pin them to the crafts with the prices written on them.

3. Store the priced crafts in boxes.

4. Decide how much to charge for admission tickets

(25 ¢ is reasonable).

5. Bring in craft supplies for making posters, announcements, and the bazaar-projects in this chapter: crayons, colored felt-tipped markers, colored paper, oaktag, poster paints, paintbrushes, paste and liquid white glue. Make each person responsible for bringing one of the craft supplies.

MEETING 3—4th Week

Old Business

All craft supplies should be on hand and ready to be used.

New Business

1. Using the appropriate supplies, make several model posters and announcements as shown in this section.

2. Hang up the completed posters and announcements and have each person make as many copies as he can during the meeting.

3. Discuss where to hang advertisements for the bazaar. Some suggestions: in school, on church bulletin boards, in stores (you must ask the store owner's permission first), and on supermarket bulletin boards. Your friends and relatives may be able to pass them along to their friends.

4. Discuss other places you might advertise: in school newspapers, the local newspaper, on radio (one of the adults will see to arranging this).

5. Assign people to hang all finished posters and announcements in the neighborhood in all designated areas.

6. Make tickets of admission (see page 272). There may be an adult in the group who can have both announcements and tickets dittoed and mimeographed for you.

7. The adults should determine what supplies you will need to decorate booths and how much the supplies will cost. Once the cost is set, the figure should be divided by the number of participants, the supplies bought and brought in the next week.

8. Assign people to bring a total of at least ten folding tables, such as bridge tables, and many folding chairs to the bazaar site. You will ready the bazaar site, if at all possible, next week.

MEETING 4—5th Week: At the Bazaar Site

Old Business

All completed posters, announcements, money for supplies, tickets, folding chairs and tables should have been brought to the bazaar site.

New Business

1. Make selling booths and a grab bag bin as described in this chapter.

2. Make games as shown in this chapter.

3. Assign persons to make the food for the bazaar, see page 278. You will have to decide how much of each kind of food you will need.

4. Discuss how you and your group will dress for the bazaar. Your parents will help you, if you choose to make costumes. Good ideas for costumes can be found in books in the library.

5. Appoint someone who will bring in a record player. Anyone who has records of ethnic music should bring them in.

6. Make any other bazaar-decorations you think necessary at this meeting or at home.

MEETING 5—A Day Before the Bazaar

Old Business

All completed things should be on hand, excluding food.

New Business

Set up booths (if the bazaar is to be held outdoors, set them up in the morning of the bazaar day). You will need at least ten booths for selling crafts and foods and for game set ups. The booth is, in effect, a decorated bridge table. You can have either a single row of booths, or a double row with an equal number of booths on each side. Alternate a craft booth, a food booth, a game booth, and so on. Space the booths about five feet apart. Make sure to have garbage cans with trash bag liners all around.

BAZAAR DAY TIPS

• Have two people at the door, one giving out the tickets by ripping along the dotted line and keeping the part that reads ADMIT ONE, and the other collecting admission money. Place the money in a cigar box. Count the ticket stubs at the end of the bazaar to see how many people came.

• If you are going to have a door prize, be sure that each ticket you sell has a different number printed on it, on both sides. Towards the end of the bazaar draw the winning number out of a hat or box and announce the winner. The winner gets a prize that has been donated previously by an adult.

• Have two people at each game booth: one to operate the game and the other to collect the money.

• Have one or two people at a craft and food booth.

• In the last half hour of the bazaar, reduce the price of all crafts by fifty per-cent.

• Money should be kept in cigar or index-card boxes at all booths and collected by an adult at the end of the bazaar.

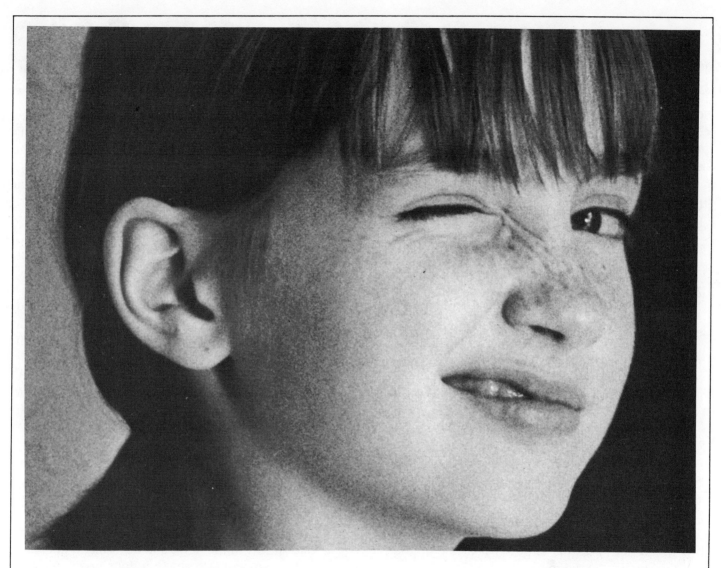

• Everyone should help clean up the bazaar area and see that all borrowed supplies are returned. The bazaar area should be left as clean as you found it.

• See the last page of this chapter for giving the money you collect to the charity or organization of your choice, and filling out the gift acknowledgement.

POSTERS AND

scissors
colored paper
paste
oaktag

crayons or colored felt-tipped
  markers
typewriter paper
pencils

POSTERS

1. Cut strips from red and white paper. Each strip should be cut a little shorter than the previous strip. Start with a red strip, then a white strip, then a red strip and so on.
2. Paste the largest red strip near the bottom of a sheet of colored oaktag.
3. Paste a red strip followed by a white strip, and so on until you have formed a pyramid of equally spaced strips. This forms the branches of the heritage tree, see illustration.
4. Make the trunk of the tree from a tall, narrow, blue paper triangle. It should be cut long enough for the bottom to extend slightly below the bottom red strip and the top a little above the top red strip, when it is pasted down.
5. Paste the triangle trunk over the branch strips.
6. Cut out stars from white paper, each a little smaller than the last.
7. Paste the stars to the trunk of the heritage tree in size order, with the largest star at the bottom, the smallest at the top.
8. Cut out green paper leaves, and paste them to the ends of the branches.
9. Write the names of the groups of people whose crafts are being sold, on the branches with crayon or colored felt-tipped marker.
10. In large letters write the words THE HERITAGE TREE BAZAAR at the bottom of the poster.
11. Write the place, date, and time of the bazaar and the admission price at the top of the poster.

ANNOUNCEMENTS

1. Draw an outline of the heritage tree on a sheet of typewriter paper just like the one on the poster. Use a pencil.
2. Color in the red bars with crayon or colored felt-tipped marker. To "draw" a white bar on white paper go over the pencil outline with a red crayon or marker.
3. Add all information you put on the poster on the announcements, plus what will be offered at the bazaar, for example, crafts, foods, games, and music. Write these things on the bottom of the announcements with a crayon or marker. Also add the name of the charity or group for which the bazaar is being held.

TICKETS

1. Cut tickets from colored paper the size of the one shown in the book and decorate as shown.
2. If you are going to have a door prize, write a number on both short and long parts of each ticket. Each ticket should have a different number on it. At the end of the bazaar, pull the winning number from a hat.

ANNOUNCEMENTS

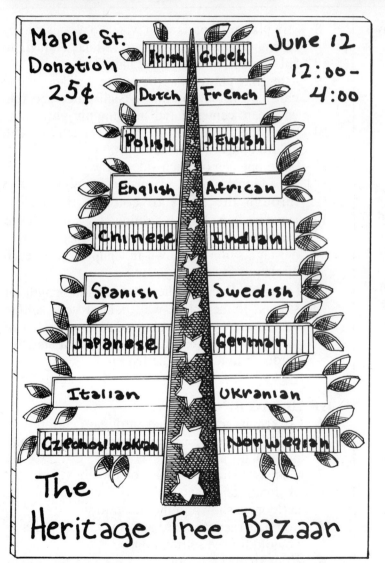

Maple St.
Donation
25¢

June 12
12:00 –
4:00

Irish · Greek
Dutch · French
Polish · Jewish
English · African
Chinese · Indian
Spanish · Swedish
Japanese · German
Italian · Ukranian
Czechoslovakian · Norwegian

The
Heritage Tree Bazaar

Come To
The First
HERITAGE
TREE
BAZAAR

June 12
12:00 – 4:00
Maple Street

Crafts · Games · Food · Music
Donation 25¢

Given for the benefit of
all the children of
the world

Heritage
Tree
Bazaar

ADMIT ONE

SELLING BOOTHS

card table
light-colored crepe paper
tape
red and white crepe
   paper streamers
scissors
colored paper
liquid white glue or
   paste

plastic drinking straws
paper puncher
two coffee cans
plaster of paris
spoon
cord
large corrugated
   cardboard carton

SELLING BOOTH

1. Cover the top of a card table with light-colored crepe paper and tape it down around the sides.
2. Open another package of crepe paper and lay the paper open on a flat surface.
3. Glue or paste a heritage tree, as described in Posters in this chapter, to the center of the opened crepe paper. Make the branches from red and white paper or from crepe paper streamers. Add a white paper star to both sides of the tree.
4. Wrap the crepe paper around the sides of the table, taping to the top of the table. The heritage tree should face front.
5. Make two poles by pinching one end of a plastic drinking straw and pushing it into another straw. Keep pinching and pushing straws into each other until you have a good-sized pole. Wooden dowels, bought where wood is sold, make a stronger pole.
6. Pinch the top straw of each pole and punch a hole through it with a paper puncher.
7. Tape green paper leaves onto both poles.

8. Mix plaster of paris with water to a consistancy resembling whipped cream. Make enough to fill two coffee cans about half full.
9. After the plaster has begun to harden in the cans, push the bottom of each pole, one into each can, centered and standing upright.
10. When the plaster has dried, cover each can with colored paper. Tape and trim.
11. Place one can on each side of the table.
12. Tie a length of cord or push a length of straws through the holes to connect the poles.
13. Make heritage flags by gluing colored circles to rectangularly shaped pieces of paper. Draw a heritage symbol, shown in Chapter 1, on each circle.
14. Tape the flags to the cord or the length of straws. If there is a wall behind your selling booth when you set it up, make a price list of the items available at the booth on a sheet of cardboard, and tape the list up.

GRAB BAG BIN

1. Cover a large corrugated cardboard carton with blue construction or crepe paper. Tape a white paper star on it, see illustration.
2. Make two straw poles as you did above, but not as long, and tape each to the back of the cartoon as shown in the illustration.
3. Add paper leaves, cord and flags to the poles as you did for the selling booth.
4. Wrap small craft objects to be sold for 50¢ in crepe paper. Put them in bin.

AND GRAB BAG BIN

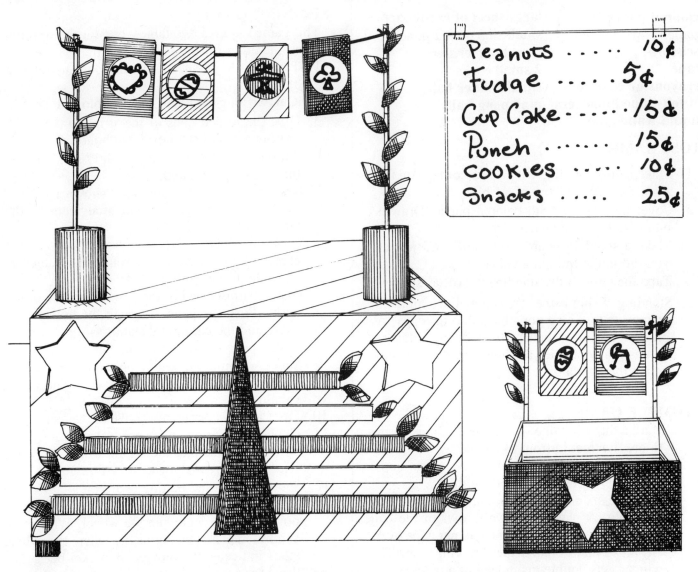

Peanuts ..... 10¢
Fudge ..... 5¢
Cup Cake ..... 15¢
Punch ..... 15¢
Cookies ..... 10¢
Snacks ..... 25¢

THREE GAMES

colored paper
paper cups
scissors
tape
crayons or colored
  felt-tipped markers
liquid white glue

large sheet of cardboard
small sharpened pencil
  without eraser
2 small corks
small rubber ball
ping pong balls

TOSS GAME

1. Make a throwing line with a piece of tape on the floor five feet in front of a table.
2. Cover paper cups with colored paper. Draw a number, 1 to 3, on each cup.
3. Make a standing board from cardboard just as you did in the Spinning Game.
4. Tape the cups to the standing board, as shown.
5. Standing behind the throwing line, players attempt to toss ping pong balls into the cups. A player gets three chances for a penny. Players win as many pennies as shown on the cup into which they get a ball.

TUMBLE GAME

1. Mark a throwing line with a piece of tape on the floor, five feet in front of a table.
2. Wrap colored paper around six paper cups.
3. Draw silly faces on each cup with crayons.
4. Stack the six cups, as shown in the drawing, on the table. A player has two throws of the ball for a nickel to topple all of the paper cups over. He must stand behind the throwing line. The winner gets double his money as a prize.

SPINNING GAME

This game requires two tables: one for the spinning wheel, the other for the betting board.
1. Tape two large sheets of cardboard together at the top.
**2. Cut two long cardboard strips. Fold ends, Fig. a.
3. Glue the folded ends of the strips to the inside bottom sides of the taped cardboard, Fig. b.
4. Cut out a cardboard circle slightly smaller than the width of the stand.
5. Draw seven heritage symbols, shown in Chapter 1, on paper circles and glue them to the large circle, equally spaced.
6. Push the small sharpened pencil through the center of the circle and through the center of one side of the cardboard stand.
7. Push the eraser end of the pencil into one of the corks. Push the pencil through the hole on the circle and the cardboard stand.
8. Push a pencil point into the other cork.
9. Squeeze liquid white glue onto the corks where they meet the pencil. Allow to dry. The wheel should spin freely.
10. Paste a red paper arrow above the wheel.
11. Cut squares out of paper. Draw the same symbols on them as are on the wheel. Tape the squares in a row to make a betting board.
12. Set the wheel and betting board on a table. The players place bets on the squares by putting down nickels. You spin the wheel. Whichever symbol the arrow points to when the wheel stops indicates the winner. A nickel bet gets a dime for a win.

SCRUMPTIOUS HERITAGE BAZAAR SNACKS

FIVE-MINUTE FUDGE

oil or butter
1 can (6 oz.) evaporated milk
⅔ cup sugar
½ teaspoon salt
½ cup chopped walnuts
1½ cups of diced
    marshmallows
1½ cups semisweet
    chocolate pieces
1 teaspoon vanilla
    extract
baking pan
medium-size saucepan
knife

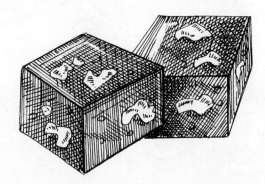

1. Grease a baking pan with oil or butter.
**2. Over medium heat, combine the evaporated milk with the sugar and salt in a medium-sized saucepan. Bring the mixture to a boil.

**3. Remove from the heat and add the remaining ingredients. Stir until the marshmallows are melted.
4. Pour the mixture into a greased baking pan and let cool.
**5. Cut the fudge into squares with a knife.

HAWAIIAN COOLER
1 can frozen pineapple-
    grapefruit juice

1 can frozen pineapple-
   orange juice
pineapple chunks
green cherries
punch bowl and ladle
1 28-oz. bottle of
   ginger ale, chilled

1. Mix the frozen juices with the amount of water stated on the labels for each can in a large punch bowl.
2. Add ginger ale to the juice.
3. Top the punch with pineapple chunks and green cherries.

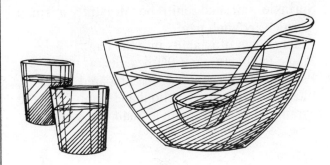

SEVEN-LAYER BARS

¼ cup (½ stick) sweet
   butter
1 cup graham cracker
   crumbs
1 cup shredded coconut
1 package (6 oz.) semi-
   sweet chocolate pieces
1 package (6 oz.)
   butterscotch pieces

1 can sweetened condensed milk
1 cup chopped nuts
saucepan
wire rack
knife

**1. Preheat oven to 350 degrees.
**2. Melt butter in a saucepan over a low heat.
  3. Pour the melted butter into a square baking pan.
  4. Sprinkle graham cracker crumbs over the melted butter and press down.
  5. Sprinkle on the coconut, then the chocolate, and then the butterscotch pieces.
  6. Pour sweetened, condensed milk evenly over all layered ingredients.
  7. Sprinkle on the nuts and press lightly.
**8. Put the baking pan into the oven and bake for thirty minutes.
**9. Remove from the oven and cool on a wire rack.
10. Cut into small bars with a knife.

INTERNATIONAL CUPCAKES
packages of
   cupcake mix
cupcake tin liners
cupcake tins

packaged white cake icing
food coloring
paper
colored felt-tipped
  markers or crayons
liquid white glue

1. Prepare the cupcake batter according to the directions on the box.
2. Put a cupcake liner into each compartment of several cupcake tins.
3. Pour batter into the cupcake tin compartments, filling each half full.

**4. Bake according to the directions on the box.
**5. Remove the cupcakes from the oven and let cool.
6. Frost the cooled cupcakes with icing prepared according to package directions. Add food coloring to white icing for different colored icings.
7. Make tiny paper flags, drawing on the symbols shown in Chapter 1. Use colored felt-tipped markers or crayons.
9. Glue flags to toothpicks and push one flag into each cupcake.

ANGRY HOT PEANUTS

canned peanuts (not
  dry-roasted)
chili powder
salt
cellophane wrap
yarn
plastic sandwich bags

1. Sprinkle salt and chili powder into a small plastic sandwich bag.
2. Empty a can of peanuts into the bag.
3. Shake the bag to coat the peanuts.
4. Put heaping teaspoons of prepared peanuts, each on a piece of cellophane wrap. Tie the wrap into a bundle with a small piece of yarn.

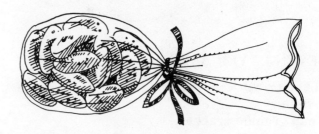

SWISS AND CHEDDAR SNACKS

cheddar and swiss cheese
knife

**3 boxes of crackers,
    different kinds**
cellophane wrap
yarn

**1. Cut cheddar and swiss cheese into thin slices
   with a knife.
2. Layer slices of cheese between three different
   kinds of crackers.
3. Wrap the cracker snacks in small pieces of
   cellophane.

4. Tie yarn around the layered snacks.

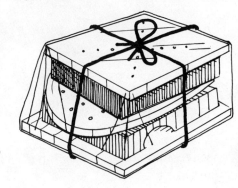

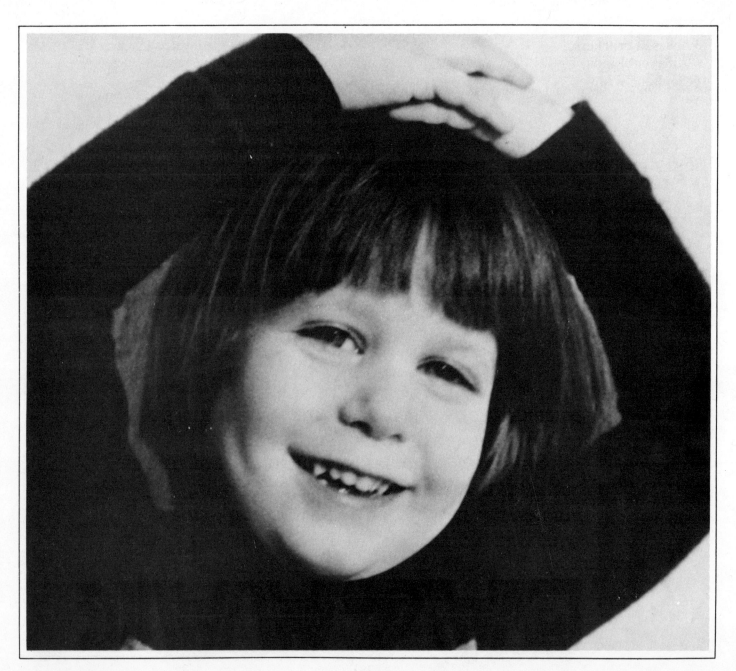

YOUR GIFT

This gift is from

1 _____

2 _____

3 _____

4 _____

who held a HERITAGE TREE BAZAAR for the benefit of all the less fortunate children of the world.

Now that the bazaar is over, it is time to send your gift of money to the group or organization of your choice. A parent will change the money into a check. Make a gift acknowledgement similar to the one shown on this page. Fill in the names of all the kids who created the bazaar. Staple your check or money order to the back of the acknowledgement. Write a letter explaining the gift and the bazaar.

Other Craft Books to Use and Have Fun With

TOYBOOK *by Steven Caney*
More Than 50 Toys to Make with Children
$3.95 paper; $8.95 cloth

PLAYBOOK *by Steven Caney*
Over 80 Spontaneous and Inventive Things to Do
Wherever Children Are
$4.95 paper; $9.95 cloth

STICKS & STONES & ICE CREAM CONES
by Phyllis Fiarotta
The Craft Book for Children
$4.95 paper; $9.95 cloth

SNIPS & SNAILS & WALNUT WHALES
by Phyllis Fiarotta
Nature Crafts for Children
$4.95 paper; $9.95 cloth

PIN IT, TACK IT, HANG IT
by Phyllis Fiarotta and Noel Fiarotta
The Big Book of Kids' Bulletin Board Ideas
$4.95 paper; $9.95 cloth

GROWING UP GREEN
by Alice Skelsey and Gloria Huckaby
Parents and Children Gardening Together
$4.95 paper; $8.95 cloth

MAKING CHILDREN'S FURNITURE AND PLAY STRUCTURES *by Bruce Palmer*
Over 50 Structures to Make from Corrugated Cardboard and Plywood
$3.95 paper; $8.95 cloth

THE KIDS' KITCHEN TAKEOVER
by Sara Bonnett Stein
Crafts, Tricks and Things to Do In—and Sometimes Out of—the Kitchen
$4.95 paper; $9.95 cloth

These books are available at local book stores or can be purchased directly from the publisher by sending a check in the amount of the book, plus 50¢ for handling and postage, to Workman Publishing Company, Inc., 231 East 51 Street, New York, New York 10022.